What former
priests and nuns
Conversations with Catholics

Conversations with Catholics will make you laugh and it will make you cry. A collection of real life stories, it illustrates both the humorous and the tragic sides of living life as a Catholic. May God use this book to bring many into the full light of the gospel.

— Bartholomew F. Brewer
Former Discalced Carmelite Priest

Conversations with Catholics is a down-to-earth account of the beliefs, hopes, doubts, and fears of the Catholic people. Loaded with practical insights from God's Word, it provides the truth that sets people free.

— Wilma Sullivan
Former Sister of Mercy

Through the mouths of Catholics, this book presents what is really going on inside the Church of Rome. Especially valuable is its warning against the dangers of ecumenism. A valuable tool for those who want to understand Catholicism, it should also be put into the hands of every Catholic priest, nun, and layman.

— Joseph Tremblay
Former Priest of the Oblates of
Mary Immaculate

This book is an excellent resource. Loaded with carefully researched information, it provides a biblical analysis of where Roman Catholicism has gone wrong. Through it you will also better understand how Catholics think and be able to explain to them the good news of Jesus Christ.

— Yvonne Freeman
Former Sister of the Holy Family

I read this book with enthusiasm and identification. Enthusiasm because the author has explained so well how the doctrines of Roman Catholicism affect the lives of the Catholic people. Identification because the many stories found in it caused me to recall my own search for God as a Catholic nun. May God bless each reader, especially those who have yet to have the veil of religion "taken away through Christ" (2 Corinthians 3:14).

— Rocio Pestaña Segovia
Former Franciscan Nun

In sharing the gospel with Catholics, I have long prayed for a book that would clearly explain the good news of Jesus Christ through stories. I thank God that such a book now exists. In *Conversations with Catholics* the reader will find the message of God's grace spoken in love. To God be the glory.

— Richard Bennett
Former Dominican Priest

Conversations with Catholics

James G. McCarthy

GOSPEL FOLIO PRESS
304 Killaly St. West, Port Colborne, ON L3K 6A6
Available in the UK from
JOHN RITCHIE LTD., Kilmarnock, Scotland

CONVERSATIONS WITH CATHOLICS

Copyright © 1997 by James G. McCarthy
This edition published by Gospel Folio Press
Port Colborne, ON L3K 6A6

Previously published by Harvest House Publishers, Eugene, OR, 1997

Library of Congress Cataloging-in-Publication Data

McCarthy, James G., 1952-
    Conversations with Catholics / James G. McCarthy
        p. cm.
    Includes bibliographical references and indexes.
    ISBN 1-88270-174-4
    1. Catholic Church—Controversial literature. I. Title.
BX1765.2.M39 1997
230'.2—dc21   97-23799
                                           CIP

Printed in the United States of America.

Contents

That Which
Fills Their Hearts

I used to think that Catholics didn't know their faith. Most couldn't explain basic doctrines such as transubstantiation, temporal punishment, or the Immaculate Conception. They seemed to have little knowledge of Roman Catholic theology and apparently no interest in learning it. Whatever formal religious education they had received dated from their childhood, and that appeared to be long-forgotten. Few read anything Catholic beyond the Sunday bulletin, typically giving it only a cursory glance.

I now see that I was wrong. Catholics do know their faith. My error stemmed from the fact that I had been applying an unfair standard. I expected Catholics to explain their beliefs with the same theological accuracy that I had become accustomed to among evangelical, Bible-believing Christians. The latter learn their faith through sermons, classes, seminars, home Bible studies, and Scripture memorization. Such Christians believe that wrong doctrine produces wrong practice, and that what you believe will determine your eternal destiny. Accordingly, they demand that teachings have a clear biblical basis, learn to express their beliefs with theological accuracy, and expect the same from other people.

None of this, however, is particularly Catholic. In Roman Catholicism it is the Church's responsibility to care for souls and to determine what is true. The primary method of teaching is neither sermons nor Bible studies. Rather, it is through *liturgy*—the public worship of the faithful—that the Catholic Church instructs its people. Teaching is not conducted in a classroom with a blackboard, but in a church gathered before an altar. There Catholics encounter the doctrines of their faith in the music, words, and actions of the priest and people.

This being the case, I have come to see that one cannot expect Catholics to express their beliefs with the same precision demanded among evangelicals. I realized this after talking to hundreds of Catholics. I discovered that when I extracted the core of what they were saying and compared it to official Roman Catholic doctrine, there was a surprisingly good correlation. Jesus taught, "The mouth speaks out of that which fills the heart" (Matthew 12:34). Theological accuracy may be lacking, but what fills the hearts of Catholics *is* the Church's teaching. Indeed, I found that laypeople often have a knack for capturing the essence of Roman Catholicism in a manner superior to that found in official documents. In contrast to the typically long, stuffy pronouncements of the learned popes and bishops, these nontheologians can summarize what Catholics believe in a simple phrase or two.

Sometime ago I began to gather these unofficial expressions of Catholicism and now present them here as *Conversations with Catholics.* This is a book about people and their beliefs as they express them, a collection of defining moments that manifest the true soul of Roman Catholicism. Here you will meet over a hundred Catholics and former Catholics. Though I have changed the names of some to protect their privacy, all are real people and their stories are based upon actual events.

This approach to explaining Catholicism is very different from that of my first book, *The Gospel According to Rome* (Harvest House, 1995). There I presented Catholicism as it is expressed in the Church's creeds and official documents. Special emphasis was given to the Vatican's recent summary of the Roman Catholic faith, the *Catechism of the Catholic Church* (1994). Consequently, *The Gospel According to Rome* is a systematic explanation of traditional, mainline Roman Catholicism.

Though the approach taken here is far less formal and rigorous, I believe that it is just as valid and leads to the same conclusions. I have sought to demonstrate this by correlating the beliefs expressed here by Catholics to the official teaching of the Church. Readers desiring further proof can obtain it by referring to the Subject Cross-Reference at the end of this book. It cross-references the topics covered here to their discussion in the *Catechism of the Catholic Church* and in *The Gospel According to Rome.*

1

"Are You Calling Me a Pharisee?"

I knew something was wrong the moment Mrs. Murphy's teenage daughter opened the door. The Murphys were a large Catholic family that I had been visiting for several weeks, trying to share the gospel. The young girl greeted me with a tense hello and a warning: "You really got my mom mad the last time you were here!"

From the tone of her voice, it was clear that the daughter had also taken offense at something I had said, but my mind was blank as to what it could be. As she led me into the living room, I quickly tried to recall my visit two weeks earlier. But the effort was unnecessary. There in the center of the room stood Mrs. Murphy. Squared-off like an aggressive boxer eager to begin a bout, she was waiting for me.

"Are you calling me a Pharisee?" Mrs. Murphy demanded.

Normally one of the sweetest persons I knew, the bite in her voice told me that she was really worked up over something.

"What do you mean?" I asked sheepishly. "I never called you a Pharisee."

With her eyes locked on me like heat-seeking missiles, Mrs. Murphy took a quick, deep breath as she prepared to launch a long-planned offensive. At the last moment, however, I was granted a stay of execution. Arrested by her normally prudent nature, Mrs. Murphy stormed out of the room in a huff.

"I'm sorry, but I don't know what you're talking about," I called after her. My plea went unheard. Mrs. Murphy was gone.

"What's this all about?" I asked her daughter.

"It was something you wrote down and gave to my mom the last time you were here. She said you called her a Pharisee."

"So that's it!" I said, finally realizing what must have happened.

During my previous visit, Mrs. Murphy and I had talked about the meaning of sin. I had tried to help her understand that she was a sinner who needed to be saved, but she would have nothing of it.

"I've lived a good and decent life," Mrs. Murphy had objected.

"The Scriptures tell us that all our righteous deeds are like a filthy garment," I answered.

"What've I ever done?"

"Have you always put God first in your life?"

"Of course!"

"Have you ever used God's name in vain?"

"No."

"Have you ever lied?"

"What would I have to lie about?"

"Have you ever stolen anything?"

"No!" she answered confidently.

"Have you ever had an unclean thought?" I asked, fully aware that I was treading on sacred ground. In Irish families, mothers with seven or more children like Mrs. Murphy are considered living saints. Predictably, she lost her patience.

"I don't know what's wrong with you. Your generation might be obsessed with sex, but I don't have those kinds of thoughts."

Realizing that the topic had progressed that day about as far as it was going to, I decided to make a tactical retreat. Taking a notepad, I wrote out a Scripture reference for Mrs. Murphy and handed it to her, asking, "Will you read this passage and see what the Bible has to say about sin?"

Mrs. Murphy, believing that she had successfully staved off my attack on her personal righteousness, accepted it cheerfully. Her warm farewell as I departed left me unprepared for the hostile reception that I was now receiving on this, my following visit.

"It wasn't me who called your mother a Pharisee," I said to Mrs. Murphy's daughter. "It was the Scriptures." I said good-bye, promising to return another day.

Deceived as to Their Sins

Mrs. Murphy is typical of a great number of Catholics. A hardworking mother living a simple life, she viewed herself as a good person. Her conscience may have troubled her from time to time, making her feel guilty about something she had said or done. But any idea that she was a sinner who had offended God and deserved eternal punishment was out of the question. Her Church, her culture, and her own heart had convinced her that, though she may not be perfect, she was ready to stand in judgment. And woe to the person who dared to say otherwise!

For some Catholics it wouldn't matter if even God Himself through His Scriptures was the one accusing them of sin. This point was illustrated to me while talking to an elderly Irishwoman. A friend and I met her while visiting farmhouses in rural County Galway, Ireland. Like Mrs. Murphy, she also claimed to have never committed a sin of any consequence. Standing at her doorstep, I opened my Bible to Romans 3:23, and holding it toward her for her to read, quoted the verse: "All have sinned and fall short of the glory of God."

"Paper doesn't refuse ink," she retorted without missing a beat. In other words, you can print what you like, but that doesn't make it so. She was no sinner regardless of who was accusing her, even God through His inspired Word.

As she slammed the door in our faces, we had a taste of how God must feel when sinners close their hearts to Him. We also had a reminder that the Roman Catholic Church has misled its people as to the most basic spiritual truth about us all: we are guilty sinners unfit to dwell in the presence of a holy God. Catholics understand neither their true spiritual condition nor the seriousness of their sins.

Sacramental Cleansing of Sin

One way that Roman Catholicism misleads its people as to their sinfulness is through the sacrament of baptism. Usually administered as soon after birth as practical, the Church teaches that this rite has two powerful effects upon a person. Baptism cleanses the soul of *original sin*, the guilt inherited from Adam. At the same time it infuses or pours *sanctifying grace* into the soul. This grace makes the individual holy and acceptable to God. The Church says that through baptism a person is born again, brought into a state of grace, made spotless and innocent before God, and becomes a member of the body of Christ.

None of this is biblical. The Scriptures teach that sinners come into a right relationship with God through personal repentance and faith in Christ (Mark 1:15; Romans 10:9-10). This involves a decision that each person must make for himself (John 1:12-13). Baptism follows as the public expression of one's commitment to Christ as Lord and Savior.

The Roman Catholic Church, on the other hand, teaches that baptism is the *cause* of spiritual rebirth. Parents can and must decide for their children. They bring their infants to the Church, the priest baptizes them and issues a baptismal certificate, and their children grow up believing that they are heaven-bound.

Consequently, when Catholics like Mrs. Murphy are told that they are sinners who need to be born again, it makes no more sense to them than it did to Nicodemus when Jesus told him the same thing (John 3:1-21). For Catholics it actually makes less sense, for according to the Church they have already been born again.

Formalized Excuses for Sin

The second way that Roman Catholicism misleads its people as to their true spiritual condition is by classifying sin into categories. Catholics are told that there are two kinds of sin: *venial* and *mortal*.

Most sins are venial; that is, pardonable infractions against God's law. They weaken one's spiritual vitality and incur a temporary form of punishment. But venial sins have no ultimate bearing on whether a person goes to heaven or not.

Mortal sins kill the life of God in a person, removing sanctifying grace from the soul. Should a person die in that condition, he would spend eternity in hell. To be forgiven of a mortal sin, a Catholic must confess it in the sacrament of confession (also called the sacrament of penance or the sacrament of reconciliation).

It is not easy, however, for an act to qualify as a mortal sin. The Church says that the sin must meet three requirements. First, it must be a big sin, *serious* or *grave* in the vocabulary of the Church. Second, the person performing the sin must be conscious that the action is grievously wrong. Finally, the individual must willfully choose to disobey God, though fully aware that God is able to help him to resist the temptation.

In practice these requirements become ready-made excuses to rationalize sin away. For example, if two people, driven by passions that they feel are beyond their control, fall into sexual immorality, the act, according to the Church, is only a venial sin. In the same way, Catholics often wink at drunkenness, arguing that a person may be struggling with a deeply rooted bad habit, breaking under pressing mental strain, or succumbing to a genetic weakness toward alcohol. If committed under such circumstances, not even a lifetime of practicing immorality or drunkenness is punishable by hell. Neither is such conduct a reason to question whether the person is truly born-again.

The Bible teaches the opposite. It says that all sins are mortal: "The wages of sin is death" (Romans 6:23). The Scriptures warn fornicators and drunkards not to deceive themselves; they will not inherit the kingdom of God unless they repent and forsake their sin (Proverbs 28:13; 1 Corinthians 6:9-10). Those who continue to practice sin should realize that they have never been born again (1 John 2:3-4; 3:4-10).

When Catholics raised with Rome's definition of sin are first exposed to what the Scriptures have to say about it, they find it unreasonable and excessively severe. Jessa Vartanian, writing in the *San Jose Mercury News*, described her first exposure to biblical preaching on sin as shocking.[1] Though raised with a solid Catholic upbringing, Vartanian stopped going to Mass during her college years, finding it somewhat meaningless. A few years later, sensing a void in her life and looking for spiritual strength, she visited an evangelical church. The minister spoke that day of his own mother, describing her as the most loving, caring, and unselfish woman he had ever known. Vartanian recounts, "The whole congregation, including me, was feeling warm and fuzzy." Then, Vartanian writes, the preacher "dropped the bombshell." He said, "But my mom isn't going to heaven."

Vartanian couldn't believe her ears:

> I held my breath. What did he mean? He'd just painted a picture of a saint. Despite being a good person, he said, his mom didn't believe Jesus Christ was her savior. And, according to him, if you didn't believe

that, no matter how wonderful a person you were, you wouldn't be taking the Up escalator.

Jessa Vartanian was equally amazed by the reaction of the congregation. Apparently no one but she was bothered by what the preacher had said. This caused her to question whether Christianity, regardless of the variety, was right for her. Since that time she has developed her own philosophy of life:

> What I've come to believe is simple: that if you live a loving, caring life with respect for yourself and others—basically, if you're a good person (and I realize my definition will differ from yours)—that you will "go to heaven," or whatever it is that happens when you die, if anything happens at all.

Though Jessa Vartanian may not realize it, what she has come to believe has much in common with what she had been taught as a child by the Roman Catholic Church: We are not defiled sinners; sin is not punishable by eternal death; and if you live a good life, you will probably go to heaven.

The preacher's text the day Vartanian visited that evangelical church may well have been "All have sinned and fall short of the glory of God" (Romans 3:23), or "The wages of sin is death" (Romans 6:23). Both are incompatible with Roman Catholic thinking.

Trivialized Punishment for Sin

Roman Catholicism further misleads its people as to the magnitude of their guilt through its teaching that sinners can make up for their sins. The Church says that when a person commits a venial or mortal sin, he stores up *temporal punishment*, which must be paid for either now here on earth or later in purgatory. In this life a Catholic can make restitution for his sins by performing voluntary *acts of penance*, such as abstaining from certain foods, saying a series of prayers, offering up his sufferings, or giving money to the poor. The individual may choose what form of penance he will perform, or, as in the sacrament of confession, a priest can assign an act of penance.

In either case the result is the same. Catholics are left thinking that sin is not that big a deal. How could it be, if saying a few prayers can make reparation for it?

When I told Tony, an easygoing Catholic, that "the wages of sin is death" (Romans 6:23), he wouldn't accept it as truth.

"That's not fair," Tony objected.

"What would be a more just sentence?" I asked.

"Seems like two weeks in hell should be enough," Tony answered, betraying what he thought about his sins.

Acts of penance also leave Catholics confused about the uniqueness and significance of Christ's sufferings on the cross. Pope John Paul II says that we all share in the redemption through our sufferings.[2] If that's the case, a Catholic might easily reason, "What's so special about Christ's sufferings?"

Ritualized Confession of Sin

Yet another way that the Roman Catholic Church leads people astray with regard to their sinfulness is by turning confession into a ritual. This takes place in various ways, the best known being the sacrament of confession. Priest and parishioner go through a well-rehearsed exchange of responses and prayers. The person lists his sins and their number of occurrences, concluding with, "I am sorry for these sins and all the sins of my whole life, especially for (here he names some past sin already confessed)." The priest then assigns the person a penance and asks him to say an Act of Contrition, a prayer expressing sorrow for sin. The priest then absolves the individual, supposedly setting him free from his sins.

The problem with ritualized confession of sin is that, like an actor in a morality play, the Catholic has been given his lines. He is not speaking to God in his own words, but is repeating a formula to a priest. All too easily this can be performed without genuine remorse or intention to change. The person departs, thinking that everything is right between him and God, when in fact he hasn't been talking to God at all.

The most common formula for confession of sin among Catholics is the Act of Contrition. Many Catholics say it daily:

> O my God, I am heartily sorry for having offended You. And I detest all my sins because of Your just punishment, but most of all because they offend You, my God, who are all good and deserving of all my love. I firmly resolve with the help of Your grace, to confess my sins, to do penance, and to amend my life. Amen.

If said from an informed mind and a sincere heart, the prayer (with the exception of the last line) is a beautiful expression of sorrow for sin. Rattled off hundreds of times each year, however, it is meaningless.

That appears to have been the case with Angela, an elderly Catholic woman dying of AIDS. I tried to explain to her that she was a sinner who needed to trust Christ as her Savior. But Angela, when talking about getting to heaven, always ended up focusing on her own good works and righteousness.

"Have you ever sinned, Angela?" I asked her on one occasion.

"Yes."

"Have you ever done anything serious enough to send you to hell?"

"No," Angela replied, calmly shaking her head in professed innocence. She knew herself to be a good Catholic. She had gone to Mass every Sunday for over 60 years, prayed the *Memorare* to Mary, and daily made an Act of Contrition. Angela had been a good wife and mother, dependable in every way. Even when life dealt her an unfair hand—she had contracted the HIV virus a few years earlier from a blood transfusion—she bore it without complaint.

Admittedly, compared to most people, Angela was a good woman. She had many admirable traits. But how did her life measure up to God's standard of righteousness as revealed in the Scriptures? That was the real issue, not how she compared to other sinners. With time running out for her, I felt I had to press the matter harder.

"Have you ever offended God?" I asked, knowing what her answer would be.

"No."

"Then why do you say the Act of Contrition?"

"What do you mean?" she asked.

"Doesn't it start, 'O my God, I am heartily sorry for having *offended You*'? Why, Angela, do you pray that almost every day, if you have never offended God?"

The poor woman had no answer. In her heart Angela was so convinced that she was a good person ready to meet God that my questions made no sense to her. Only God knows if her daily Act of Contrition amounted to anything more than the repetition of holy poetry. From my conversations with Angela, I could only conclude that she had repeated the prayer so many times that the words had lost their meaning.

The prayer continues: "And I detest all my sins because of Your just punishment, but most of all because *they offend You, my God*, who are all good and deserving of all my love."

These are commendable sentiments when spoken from the heart of a truly repentant sinner. But they are meaningless when coming from the lips of a person who actually believes the very opposite. Angela, at least as far as she was concerned, had never offended God. She wasn't heartily sorry. Neither did she detest all her sins. Like many Catholics, she probably didn't even know what the word *contrition* means.

I always marveled how Angela also denied that she had AIDS, despite testing HIV-positive and having every classic symptom of the disease. Her fingernails were distorted from a fungal infection and her skin scarred where cancerous cells had been removed. Each day her nurses had to swab her mouth with medicine to keep ever-threatening thrush at bay. Once a vibrant woman, she was now a frail invalid, her lungs clogged with pneumonia. Her immune system's T-cell count was at 16 (about 1200 is normal). Yet to the day she died, Angela refused to accept her doctors' diagnosis.

It can be the same with Catholics and their sin. Deceived by the lie of self-righteousness, they cannot see their sin despite clear evidence to the contrary. Sadly, many will understand the magnitude of their guilt only when they stand in judgment, naked and ashamed before God in His holiness. Only then will they know that "all have sinned and fall short of the glory of God" (Romans 3:23).

Deluded as to Their Sins

Being baptized, receiving the sacrament of confession, and saying the Act of Contrition are no substitutes for repenting and trusting Christ to save us. God wants internal, not external brokenness. "Rend your heart and not your garments" (Joel 2:13), says the Lord. David wrote, "A broken and a contrite heart, O God, Thou wilt not despise" (Psalm 51:17). David knew what he was talking about. After committing adultery with Bathsheba and arranging for the murder of her husband, David was rebuked by the Lord through the prophet Nathan saying, "Why have you despised the word of the Lord by doing evil in His sight?" (2 Samuel 12:9). David, crushed under the guilt of his sin, cried out to God:

> Against Thee, Thee only, I have sinned,
> And done what is evil in Thy sight,
> So that Thou art justified when Thou dost speak,
> And blameless when Thou dost judge (Psalm 51:4).

David allowed God's Word to judge his innermost being. Speaking of God's rebuke, he wrote, "Thine arrows have sunk deep into me, and Thy hand has pressed down on me" (Psalm 38:2). Overcome by his personal guilt, he confessed his sin directly to God:

> I acknowledged my sin to Thee,
> And my iniquity I did not hide;
> I said, "I will confess my transgressions to the Lord";
> And Thou didst forgive the guilt of my sin (Psalm 32:5).

Unlike David, most Catholics think that the majority of their sins have no eternal bearing on their soul, and so dismiss them as unimportant. I spoke to one Catholic woman in her fifties who was only willing to admit to having committed 20 sins over the span of her life. Others, like Mrs. Murphy, can't recall a single sin. Misled by the Church, these people are living under a delusion. How else could someone like Mrs. Murphy claim to be without sin, and yet weekly participate at Mass in the Penitential Rite? One of the prayers recited by Catholics during this rite reads:

> I confess to almighty God, and to you, my brothers and sisters, that I have sinned through my own fault in my thoughts and in my words, in what I have done, and in what I have failed to do; and I ask blessed Mary, ever virgin, all the angels and saints, and you, my brothers and sisters, to pray for me to the Lord our God.[3]

At Mass on the Sunday before I visited Mrs. Murphy, she had repeated this confession of guilt along with the priest. As she did, she softly struck her breast with her fist as instructed by the liturgy. This expression of sorrow over sin has its roots in the very passage of the Bible that I had asked Mrs. Murphy to read and at which she took such offense. It is the parable that Jesus told "to certain ones who trusted in themselves that they were righteous, and viewed others with contempt" (Luke 18:9). It was written to people just like Mrs. Murphy.

> Two men went up into the temple to pray, one a Pharisee, and the other a tax-gatherer. The Pharisee stood and was praying thus to himself, "God, I thank Thee that I am not like other people: swindlers, unjust, adulterers, or even like this tax-gatherer. I fast twice a

week; I pay tithes of all that I get." But the tax-gatherer, standing some distance away, was even unwilling to lift up his eyes to heaven, but was beating his breast, saying, "God, be merciful to me, the sinner!" I tell you, this man went down to his house justified rather than the other; for everyone who exalts himself shall be humbled, but he who humbles himself shall be exalted (Luke 18:10-14).

God used this portion of Scripture to help Mrs. Murphy see herself as He saw her. And though at first she took offense, later she repented. Having come to understand the full magnitude of her sin, she trusted Christ as her only hope of salvation.

2

"Give Me the Works, Father"

From a pew near the front of Saint Julia's Catholic Church, I watched the pallbearers roll Marie's casket slowly down the center isle. It was a sad occasion. I had known Marie for many years and had tried to share the good news of Jesus Christ with her. I had given her a Bible and encouraged her to read the Gospel of John.

Marie said that she believed in Christ, but I had my doubts. Not that she didn't believe in Jesus in a historical sense. All Catholics do. What I questioned was whether or not she was trusting Christ to save her in a personal sense. Whenever I asked Marie about her hope of salvation, she would always respond with a confused mixture of Christ and self, faith and works, grace and merit. She never opened the Bible that I gave her. She never seemed to want to talk about the Lord. Nevertheless, when a person is dying, one hopes for the best, knowing God to be gracious and merciful.

"Marie wasn't afraid to die," said Father Harry, the parish priest, during her eulogy. "I remember how on my last visit to see Marie, she greeted me as I entered her room. Then, looking me straight in the eye, she said, 'I know I'm dying. I have only a short time to live. Give me the works, Father.'"

Marie, in Father Harry's opinion, was a model of how a Christian should face death. I thought the opposite, what little confidence I had that she might personally know Christ vanishing with the eulogy. Marie's dying hope, it appeared, rested in three rituals: confession, communion, and the anointing of the sick—the trilogy of sacraments known as the Last Rites—"the works," as she put it.

Why would a dying Catholic's last request be for a series of rituals? Because Rome has taught its people to approach God not directly, but through the sacraments of the Church.

Grace Dispensers

Roman Catholicism teaches that Christ established seven sacraments: baptism, penance, Eucharist, confirmation, matrimony, holy orders, and anointing of the sick. Each is a channel of a supernatural gift from God called grace. Available because of the merits of Christ, grace is the indispensable and necessary means of salvation and sanctification.

According to the Church, the sacraments dispense two kinds of grace: *sanctifying grace* and *actual grace*. Sanctifying grace gives a person a participation in the divine life of God. Initially poured into a person's soul through the sacrament of baptism, sanctifying grace makes an individual holy and acceptable to God, pleasing in His sight. It remains with the person as long as the individual does not commit a mortal sin.

Actual grace is a helping hand from God to do good and avoid evil. It helps a person to perform a specific good deed or act. Because this grace passes with its using, the Church teaches that Catholics must continually obtain additional actual grace by regularly receiving the sacraments.

In order for a sacrament to effectively dispense grace, the minister conducting it must follow a precisely defined ceremony called a *rite*. Established by the Church, each rite describes the words and actions of both the minister and the participants.

According to Catholic theology, the sacraments dispense grace *by the ritual being conducted*. This means that the words and actions of the minister of the sacrament do not merely symbolize or commemorate blessings that the people have already received or are about to receive from God. Rather, the sacrament dispenses grace as the ritual is conducted, "by the very fact of the action's being performed."[4]

This supernatural effect occurs, says the Church, whenever the rite is properly executed, regardless of the spiritual condition of the deacon, priest, or bishop conducting the ritual. In other words, even if the minister is far from God and deep in sin himself, the sacramental rite still produces its intended effect.

How is this doctrine applied in everyday Catholicism? Consider, for example, the case of the pastor of one of the largest Catholic parishes in San Francisco.[5] Eleven men accused him of having sexually molested them when they were boys. In March of 1994, following an investigation, the bishop of San Francisco relieved the priest of his duties. The following year the San Francisco district attorney's office brought criminal charges against the same priest, charging him with having embezzled $251,000 from Catholic parishioners and from the Church.

If these offenses did in fact occur, would the debauched condition of the priest invalidate the thousands of sacraments performed by him during the two decades that the crimes spanned? Did parishioners whose children had been baptized by him begin inquiring whether their children should be rebaptized? Did those who had given money for Masses to be said for their deceased relatives in purgatory start asking for refunds? Did Catholics who had confessed their sins to the priest begin to wonder if their transgressions had really been absolved?

Not at all. As we have seen, Roman Catholicism teaches that sacramental grace is dispensed *from the work performed*. The ability of a rite to confer grace is independent of the spiritual condition of the minister who performs it. Consequently, the sacraments this priest administered are valid. In fact, despite over 400 allegations of pedophilia against priests in the United States over the last decade, no one has questioned the validity of any of the sacraments that the accused performed.

One of the most shameless applications of this Roman Catholic doctrine rocked Ireland in November of 1994. A 68-year-old Roman Catholic priest had a heart attack while visiting the Incognito, a gay bathhouse in Dublin that advertises itself as "Ireland's most famous male-only sauna club." Responding to calls for help, two other Catholic priests emerged from private rooms in the club to give the dying man the Last Rites.[6]

One must ask, Is this Christianity? Would the Church have us believe that two men, interrupted in their homosexual activities, can benefit a third man dying on the tiled floor of a gay bathhouse by performing rituals over him?

At question is not whether God would be willing to forgive a repentant sinner who cries out with his last breath for Jesus to save him. Rather, the question is, Are Catholic rites so powerful that they can channel God's grace to people even when the priest administering the rite is living an outright lie? And even more to the point, Is Christian salvation and sanctification to be found in rites at all?

The Bible answers no to both of these questions. God is holy. He hates religious hypocrisy. When the people of Israel defiled themselves with the sins of the Canaanites, God told them,

> Bring your worthless offerings no longer,
> Incense is an abomination to Me.

New moon and sabbath, the calling of assemblies—
I cannot endure iniquity and the solemn assembly.
I hate your new moon festivals and your appointed
    feasts,
They have become a burden to Me.
I am weary of bearing them (Isaiah 1:13-14).

When the Jews, God's people of the Old Testament, continued in their religious hypocrisy, the Lord proclaimed, "Oh that there were one among you who would shut the gates, that you might not uselessly kindle fire on My altar!" (Malachi 1:10). Likewise, God requires His New Testament people to worship Him "in spirit and truth" (John 4:24). He demands integrity. He desires spiritual worship from the hearts of obedient people. The salvation that He offers is not found in rituals but in a relationship: "peace with God through our Lord Jesus Christ" (Romans 5:1). God's adopted children stand in His grace (Romans 5:2); they have no need of sacraments to channel grace to them. Their access to the Father is not through a priest but through the Son and in the Spirit (Ephesians 2:18).

Mechanical Worship

What has the ritualistic focus of Roman Catholicism produced? The results can be seen in the way that Catholics pray. They don't *speak* to God in prayer. Rather, they *say* their prayers, typically repeating them by rote or reading them from a prayer book. The Church supplies ready-made prayers for every occasion: for the living, for the dead; before receiving communion, after receiving communion; morning prayers, evening prayers; before meals, after meals; to confess sin; to honor Mary; and so on.

The Church also writes the prayers to be recited by the priest during the Mass. Official liturgy instructs the priest when to kneel, bow, raise his hands, and speak. He is told what to say and how to say it. Innovation is strictly forbidden for, if the rite is to produce its intended effect, all essential elements of the ritual must be performed precisely.

The Church also scripts the participation of the laity in Sunday worship. The liturgy instructs the congregation when to stand, sit, kneel, cross themselves, and say *Amen*. In this manner it guides both people and priest through the Introductory Rites, the Liturgy of the Word, the Liturgy of the Eucharist, the Communion Rite, and the Concluding Rite.

Not even attendance at Sunday Mass is voluntary. The Church teaches that on "Sundays and other holy days of obligation the faithful are bound to participate in the Mass."[7] The number of holy days of obligation varies among countries. In the United States there are six. Two honor Christ: Christmas (December 25) and His ascension (40 days after Easter). Three honor Mary: the Solemnity of Mary the Mother of God (January 1); the Assumption of Mary into Heaven (August 15); and the Immaculate Conception of Blessed Mary the Virgin (December 8). One honors the saints: All Saints' Day (November 1). Failure to attend Mass on Sunday or a holy day of obligation may constitute a mortal sin.

The effects of this regimented and mandatory worship can be seen in how some Catholics talk about going to Mass. In 1970 the Church began allowing Catholics to fulfill their obligation to attend Mass "either on the holy day or on the evening of the preceding day."[8] Since then, most parishes have offered a "Sunday Vigil Mass" on Saturday evening at 5:00 or 5:30 P.M. Well attended, Sunday Mass on Saturday is seen as a good way of "getting it over with," in the words of some Catholics. Early Sunday-morning Masses are popular with the young who don't want Mass to "wreck the whole day," as some put it. Later Sunday Masses, like the ones at noon, have a reputation of "dragging on forever." They are for the elderly and those who, having been up late the night before, couldn't get out of bed any earlier.

Activity at the back door of the church is also revealing. With attendance mandatory and defiant disobedience a mortal sin, you can be sure that someone has asked, "What if I arrive five minutes late? Is my attendance still valid? What if I decide to leave early? Have I met my obligation?" Opinion varies among Catholics as to how late one can arrive and still have the Mass "count." Some say you must arrive before the reading of the Gospel, about ten minutes into the Mass. Others say that attendance is valid as long as you arrive before the Eucharistic prayer, about 30 minutes into the Sunday Mass. All agree that you must remain until the Communion Rite, about seven minutes from the end of Mass.

So what do some Catholics do? They routinely arrive late and leave early. It is not uncommon for some Catholics to walk right out the back door after receiving communion rather than to return to their pew for the Concluding Rite. Having punched their spiritual time clock for the week, they leave as soon as legally allowed by the Church. Even Catholics who stay for the whole thing often comment, "I don't get anything out of it." One could only guess what percentage of Catholics would attend Sunday Mass if it wasn't mandatory.

The detrimental effects of obligatory ritualistic worship can also be seen on the faces of Catholics at Mass. Most, having sat through the ceremony a thousand times before, find it hard to keep their minds from drifting. Trying to add some variety to the rite, the Church rotates portions of the liturgy each week according to a liturgical calendar. Following these changes in the printed guides to the Mass, however, requires that parishioners flip back and forth between standard and rotated portions—a practice not easily mastered. Most Catholics don't even try, having concluded that the benefits are not worth the effort. Only a small portion of the congregation participates in singing the hymns or making the liturgical responses. A recent religious bestseller by Thomas Day titled *Why Catholics Can't Sing* highlighted the widely accepted fact among Catholics that worship at Mass is flat. Day, himself a Catholic, writes:

I would just like to know why congregational singing in Catholic parishes generally does not seem to have any zest at all. Why are all those people staring into space, when they're supposed to be singing?[9]

Day cites a University of Notre Dame study conducted between 1984 and 1989 of parishes in the United States that backs up his observation. Though there were some exceptions, overall researchers found participation "mechanical and listless."[10] "Rarely was there an atmosphere of deeply prayerful involvement," reported Mark Searle, one of the authors of the *Notre Dame Study.*[11]

Proponents of the Mass argue that the rite has a solid scriptural basis and that much of the wording is taken directly from the Bible. They also point out that the Scriptures are read at every Mass. Those who get nothing out of the Mass, they say, have no one to blame but themselves.

The Scriptures, however, have to be used properly if they are to lead people to the true worship of God. This is where the Mass fails. Despite the biblical origins of some of its wording, the liturgy of the Mass is filled with false teaching. And though the Scriptures are read during the Mass—usually a passage from the Old Testament, a selection from the Epistles, and a portion from the Gospels—Catholics don't learn the Bible by attending Mass. Part of the problem is that the Church determines what passages will be read each week, publishing a three-year rotation that chops the Scriptures into bite-size portions. This all but destroys the context. A short sermon called a homily follows the third reading. It typically consists of 12 minutes of moralizing, storytelling, or fundraising by a priest or deacon. Some priests try to teach the Scriptures but, unsaved and lacking the anointing of the Spirit, they don't understand God's Word themselves. The Bible teaches that "a natural man does not accept the things of the Spirit of God; for they are foolishness to him, and he cannot understand them, because they are spiritually appraised" (1 Corinthians 2:14). When on rare occasion a priest trusts Christ, is born again, and starts to preach the truth, people immediately notice the difference. So does the bishop's office, and the believing priest is either silenced or forced out.

Impersonal Relationships

The way Catholics interact with one another before and after the Mass also says something about the quality of their worship. They file into church with no more affinity toward one another than commuters catching a train. School friends and neighbors may greet each other, but that's the limit.

I remember a weekend when I was still a Catholic that my wife, Jean, and I spent with Father Barry, a good friend. He was the pastor of three rural parishes, each separated by about an hour's drive. After Sunday-morning Mass at the primary parish, we traveled with Father Barry to the next town so that he could say Sunday Mass there. When we arrived, about 30 parishioners were waiting on the steps of the small church. A few greeted Father Barry as he unlocked the church doors and turned on the lights. He then excused himself to put on his vestments for Mass.

No one asked Jean or me who we were or why we were visiting their church. Everyone just filed into the pews and waited for Mass to begin.

Jean and I were just as bad. Accustomed to the impersonal coldness of our big-city parish, we didn't go out of our way to greet anyone either. Nevertheless, even at the time it seemed odd to us that way out in the countryside a group of Catholics such as ourselves could be so indifferent toward one another.

This feeling only intensified when in the latter part of the Mass during the Communion Rite we came to the "sign of peace." That is when, as instructed by the liturgy, Catholics express their unity and love for one another.

"The peace of the Lord be with you always," said Father Barry, his hands extended above the altar.

"And also with you," we answered in unison with the congregation.

"Let us offer each other the sign of peace."

As directed by the liturgy, we each dutifully shook hands with the people around us, offering one another the standard greeting: "Peace be with you."

What did this liturgical greeting mean to us? Not much. Everyone was simply going through the motions as required by the rite. What did our liturgical worship mean to God? Probably not much more. The words of the rite were repeated in the same dull tones to which Catholics everywhere are accustomed.

The way we related toward one another as Catholics reflected how we related to God. The Bible teaches that one cannot worship God from the heart and at the same time be coldhearted toward God's people: "Whoever loves the Father loves the child born of Him" (1 John 5:1), and again, "The one who loves God should love his brother also" (1 John 4:21).

When Jean and I initially encountered the love that born-again Christians have for one another, it took some getting used to. Not only did the Christians at the first evangelical church we visited warmly greet us, but one family invited us to their home for lunch. Such hospitality was unknown in the Catholicism with which we were familiar.

It also surprised me how many people returned for the Sunday evening service. Attendance wasn't required; they wanted to be there. When the meeting was over, they lingered, often for up to an hour, enjoying fellowship with one another. In the weeks that followed I learned that it wasn't unusual for the custodian to start flicking the lights off and on to encourage people to leave. "Don't you have homes to go to?" he would tease in good-hearted jesting. Like many Catholics, we were accustomed to evacuating the church as soon as Mass was over as if in a fire drill.

The thing that struck me most about these Christians was the way they would speak about the Lord. They expressed love and appreciation for Him as naturally as they would talk about a member of their family—because He *was* a member. They knew the Lord and loved Him. Their corporate worship was the overflow of that relationship. Reciting prayers was out of the question. All worship was spontaneous. Singing was heartfelt and enthusiastic.

Catholics seldom talk about the Lord. I remember discussing this with James, a Catholic deacon and graduate of a Catholic seminary. He told me that if anyone in his theology classes had dared to speak about love for Jesus, that person would have been "laughed out of the school." Theological, philosophical, social, and political discussions were fine. Just don't get personal about God. The same is true about Catholics in general. They will talk about their priest, the pope, religious practices, and moral and social issues. But in all my years as a Catholic, I can't recall anyone initiating a conversation about the Lord. I have never heard a priest or nun talk about the Lord Jesus in a personal way.

One exception was Sister Brid. For a time she came to a Bible study that I was teaching. Brid lived in a convent with 28 other nuns. Yet she told me that when she wanted to talk about the Lord, she had to come to our study. In the convent, she said, Jesus' name was never mentioned, except when saying prayers or as part of the liturgy.

It's like that in many Catholic homes. Jesus is a stranger who resides in the tabernacle of the local Catholic Church. You genuflect before Him. You say your prayers to Him. But He is as distant as an uncle you have never met who lives in a far-off country. To speak about Jesus with affection around family members would be an embarrassment to all.

Catholics excuse their silence, claiming that their relationship with the Lord is too private to discuss. But the fact of the matter is that it is too nonexistent to discuss. They don't talk about Him because they have nothing to say.

Much of the blame for this can be laid at the door of the Roman Catholic Church. It has misled its people, giving them rites instead of a relationship, sacraments instead of a Savior. Consequently, when death draws near, they, like my friend Marie, call not on the Lord to save them, but for a priest to give them "the works." In Father Harry's eulogy, there was no mention of the *Worker*, the Lord Jesus, who gave His life for us on the cross. There was no reference to His finished work or of God's free offer of salvation. No, the priest gave Marie what she wanted, "the works," and she died peacefully a few days later, thinking she was right with God. As with so many Catholics, the sacraments of the Church had lulled her into a false confidence, and she quietly slipped into the next life and the judgment that awaits.

3

"Nobody Knows"

After we trusted Christ and left the Catholic Church in our mid-twenties, the Lord began preparing Jean and me to serve Him. During this time of training, we often had the pleasure of accompanying Mr. O. Jean Gibson, a gifted Bible teacher and evangelist, in visiting the homes of Catholics. The most memorable occasion was the night we called on John and Jane DeLisi. Disenchanted with the Roman Catholic Church, the DeLisis had begun looking elsewhere for answers. One Sunday morning they visited the church where Mr. Gibson was an elder and frequent preacher.

The DeLisis liked what they found. They noted that when Mr. Gibson spoke that day, his teaching came directly out of the Bible. They also liked the lack of ritual: the standing up, sitting down, kneeling, and repetitive responses of which they had grown so tired during their almost 30 years as Catholics. Wanting to learn more about this new church, the DeLisis accepted an offer of a visit.

When Mr. Gibson, Jean, and I arrived at the DeLisis' home one evening a few days later, John and Jane introduced us to a second Catholic couple, Roger and Beverly. They also were searching for answers. And so the seven of us crowded into the DeLisis' apartment living room for what turned out to be an evening that none of us will forget.

Sensing that the DeLisis and their friends were somewhat apprehensive, Mr. Gibson set about putting them at ease. Taking a seat in an overstuffed chair, he slid off his loafers. Then in the down-home drawl of his native Texas, he engaged in friendly conversation, inquiring about the two couples' backgrounds and spiritual interests.

Then it was time to get down to business. As casual as someone asking for the time, Mr. Gibson posed one of life's most important questions to the two Catholic couples. "If you were to die tonight," he asked, "what do you think would happen to you?"

The room went still. None of the four were prepared for such a forthright and portentous question. As Catholics it wasn't the sort of thing they talked about. One's final destiny was part of the great unknown, best left alone.

Finally, Jane DeLisi broke the silence. "Nobody knows. How could you know?"

"Well," Mr. Gibson replied, "would you like to know if you're going to heaven?"

Again it was Jane who answered. "You can't know. Nobody knows, not even the pope."

"Let me show you something from the Bible," Mr. Gibson offered. "It says that you can *know* that you are going to heaven." He turned to 1 John 5:13 in his Bible and asked Jane, who by then had established herself as the group's spokesperson, to read it aloud.

Taking the Bible in her hands, Jane began, "These things I have written to you who believe in the name of the Son of God, in order that you may have eternal life." When she finished, she looked up as if to say, "So what?"

Mr. Gibson looked equally puzzled. Taking the Bible from her, he took a quick glance at the verse, then returning it to Jane, said, "Read it again."

"These things I have written to you," Jane read, "who believe in the name of the Son of God, in order that you may have eternal life." She continued staring at the verse, trying to figure out what Mr. Gibson thought was so significant about it.

"Try it once more," Mr. Gibson asked.

Again Jane read 1 John 5:13, this time somewhat slower. "These things I have written to you who believe in the name of the Son of God"—she paused long enough to see if Mr. Gibson had any objections, and then continued—"in order that you may have eternal life."

"You're leaving out part of the verse."

"I am?" Jane was baffled. An experienced teacher with eight years' experience in the Catholic parochial school system, she taught reading! Now her visitor was telling her that, despite three attempts, she couldn't get a simple sentence straight. Not easily deterred, Jane gave it another try.

"These things I have written to you who believe in the name of the Son of God, in order that you may have eternal life." Jane, knowing that she had read the verse the same way once more, decided not to wait to be corrected. "I don't see it," she complained. "What's the problem? What am I doing wrong?"

"You're leaving out the word *know*. Isn't the word *know* in the verse?"

Jane took another look, and with a smile confessed, "Yes, it is. I can't see how I could have missed it, but there it is."

"OK, well, read it—the whole verse."

"'These things I have written to you who believe in the name of the Son of God, in order *that you may know* that you have eternal life.' That is different. I see your point. I didn't think that anyone could *know* that they were going to heaven."

"Who does the verse say may know?" Mr. Gibson asked.

"You who believe in the name of the Son of God," Jane read.

"That's right. And do you know what it means to 'believe in the name of the Son of God'?"

"I'm not sure."

"Well, let me show you."

For the next 90 minutes, Mr. Gibson explained the gospel to the four Catholics. When he finished, John, Jane, Roger, and Beverly were ready to trust the Savior. We all got down on our knees and, one by one, they each spoke to God, telling Him of their decision to repent and trust Jesus to save them.

Why Jane Can't Read

Undoubtedly, Jane was nervous the evening she misread 1 John 5:13 four times. It is also true that the wording of the verse is somewhat awkward. But I think the main reason that she had so much difficulty reading it had to do with *what* the verse says. The idea that anyone could know that he or she was going to heaven was so foreign to her thinking that Jane simply skipped over that part of the verse. She read it the way she expected it to read, making it say what she believed to be true.

Like Jane, most Catholics are unsure about what will happen to them in the next life. This was vividly demonstrated to me when filming *Catholicism: Crisis of Faith*, a documentary examining the teachings of Roman Catholicism. We set up our camera outside Saint Patrick's Cathedral in New York City. There we interviewed Catholics leaving Mass. We asked them how they hoped to get to heaven and whether they thought that they were going to make it.

"I sure hope so," Jack, a Catholic from North Dakota, answered.

Catherine, Jack's wife, agreed. "I hope so, too. But there will be someone else judging that."

"Everybody hopes," a woman from France told us. "Every Catholic hopes."

"You don't know what's going to happen when you get there," Norman, a resident of New York City, explained. "You might find a surprise waiting for you."

Joe from Baltimore was also visiting the cathedral that day. When we asked him if he expected to go to heaven, he answered, "I hope to. Yes, I expect to. And I hope to. My wife is, I hope, up there. She died about two years ago."

When we asked Joe whether he *knew* he was going to heaven, he made an important distinction. "No," he answered. "I don't know. But I hope to. I don't think you know what is going on in the future. We only hope that we wind up in heaven. That's what we strive for."

Hoping, but not *knowing*, is the consensus among Catholics. Cardinal John O'Connor, outside whose cathedral we conducted these interviews, has said as much himself:

> Church teaching is that I don't know, at any given moment, what my eternal future will be. I can hope, pray, do my very best—but I still don't know. Pope John Paul II doesn't know absolutely that he will go to heaven, nor does Mother Teresa of Calcutta.[12]

I once heard a Catholic woman compare salvation to a bank account. You open the account when you are baptized. Receiving the sacraments and performing good works is like adding money to your account. Committing a venial sin takes money out. A mortal sin bankrupts your account. In order to restore it to a positive balance, you must receive the sacrament of confession. Whether you go to heaven or hell is determined by the status of your account at the moment of death. If you have money in the bank, you go to heaven. If not, you don't. And since nobody knows what his final balance will be, no one can know where he is going until he gets there.

Why Catholics Don't Know

From the day that a Catholic is baptized until the day he dies, he is on probation with God. Life is a trial during which he must prove by his faith and obedience that he is worthy of heaven. His eternal salvation hangs in the balance. That's what the Catholics we interviewed outside Saint Patrick's Cathedral told us when we asked them *how* they hoped to get to heaven.

"I hope to get to heaven," Julia, a Catholic woman coming out of the cathedral, told us, "by leading a good life and being honest with people."

Norman gave us a list of requirements to get to heaven: ". . . prayer, and perseverance, and by doing what the Catholic Church teaches. Be honest. Do good. Go to confession. Go to church. And treat your neighbors as good as you can."

Sharon from New York state also spoke of salvation as the accomplishment of a list of activities: "doing good works, believing in Jesus Christ, trying to practice your beliefs and your religion in your everyday life, doing things for humanity."

Joyce from Michigan summarized the requirements as: "Follow your Ten Commandments . . . live a good Christian life, love everyone."

Did these Catholics think that they could accomplish these things well enough to get into heaven? Most admitted that they weren't so sure.

"Well, I got a lot of work to do," Ray, a Catholic from Ohio, told us. "I hope to go to heaven when I die. I hope and pray to God that I do. And if I don't, I know I did something I shouldn't have done."

"I hope the good things I do on earth will sit well with God and He'll look favorably on it and take me into heaven," said Fran, a Catholic from Seneca Falls, New York.

"If you did right you'll get there," another man explained. "If you haven't done right by your Man, you'll get your just rewards, maybe in hell, maybe in purgatory."

The Catholic belief that entrance into heaven is the reward for good works performed on earth is expressed at every Catholic funeral. One of the suggested readings in the funeral liturgy is from the Book of Wisdom, part of the collection of books that the Catholic Church claims is part of the Old Testament. With reference to the deceased person, the minister reads, "Afflicted in a few things, in many they shall be well rewarded: because God hath tried them, and found them worthy of himself" (Wisdom 3:1-5).

The inspired Scriptures speak to the contrary. They say that "there is none righteous, not even one. . . . There is none who does good, not even one" (Romans 3:10-12). In the day of judgment, God will find none worthy of Himself. It is only in Christ that we can find acceptance before a holy God (Ephesians 1:3-8; Jude 24).

In Catholicism, the individual himself must stand before God in judgment and be found worthy of eternal life. Entrance into heaven is a merited reward. This is expressed throughout the funeral liturgy. For example, there is a selection of 47 prayers provided to tailor the funeral rite to the particular circumstances of the deceased. These include prayers for the person who has died after a long illness, one who died suddenly, an elderly person, a young person, a baptized child, and a child who died before baptism. The minister chooses the prayer that is most appropriate. If the deceased (we'll call him John) had been a Catholic priest, the liturgy instructs the minister conducting the funeral to pray:

> Lord God, you chose our brother John to serve your people as a priest and to share the joys and burdens of their lives. Look with mercy on him and give him the reward of his labors, the fullness of life promised to those who preach your holy Gospel. We ask this through Christ our Lord. Amen.[13]

This prayer asks God to give the deceased priest what he deserves: "the reward of his labors." His recompense should be "the fullness of life."

Should the deceased be even more deserving—a bishop, for example—the liturgy instructs the minister to pray:

> Almighty and merciful God, eternal Shepherd of your people, listen to our prayers and grant that your servant John, our bishop, to whom you entrusted the care of this Church, may enter the joy of his eternal Master, there to receive the rich reward of his labors. We ask this through Christ our Lord. Amen.[14]

This is another give-him-what-he-deserves prayer. It asks God to grant the deceased bishop entrance into heaven based on "his labors."

The same kind of prayer is found in the funeral rite of a pope:

> O God, from whom the just receive an unfailing reward, grant that your servant John, our Pope, whom you made vicar of Peter and shepherd of your Church, may rejoice forever in the vision of your glory, for he was a faithful steward here on earth of the mysteries of your forgiveness and grace. We ask this through Christ our Lord. Amen.[15]

This prayer asks God to give the deceased pope the reward of rejoicing forever "in the vision of your glory." The pope should receive this privilege because he "was a faithful steward here on earth."

One might wonder what the writers of the liturgy would do if called upon to compose a prayer for a deceased Catholic who was known by all to be a poor lost sinner with no merits of his own. The funeral liturgy actually provides one such prayer—prayer number 44. It is for the person who has ended his life by his own hand. The Church considers suicide to be a serious and potentially mortal sin that incurs eternal punishment. Under the Code of Canon Law that was in effect until 1983, a Catholic who committed suicide was denied a Church burial. Since then the Church has taken a more sympathetic view and has lifted the ban. Nevertheless, in composing a prayer for the one who has taken his own life, the Church realized the deceased would have only one possible hope of salvation. And what might that be?

> God, lover of souls, you hold dear what you have made and spare all things, for they are yours. Look gently on your servant John, and by the blood of the cross forgive his sins and failings.

Amazing! Prayer 44 drops all pretense that the deceased deserves to go to heaven or has any claim to eternal life based upon his own merits. Apparently, even Rome realizes that the only hope of salvation for a genuine sinner is to plead the blood of Christ—the biblical basis of salvation. In the liturgy, however, prayer 44 is the exception, not the rule, for Rome fails to realize that we are all lost sinners who must trust Christ, and Him alone, if we are to be saved.

What About Jesus?

There are many references in the Catholic funeral liturgy to the work of Christ. For example, in the opening prayer the minister says of the deceased (we'll again call him John),

> O God, glory of believers and life of the just, by the death and resurrection of your Son, we are redeemed: have mercy on your servant John, and make him worthy to share the joys of paradise, for he believed in the resurrection of the dead. We ask this through Christ our Lord.[16]

Christ, however, is not presented in the Church's liturgy as the victorious Savior who guarantees the salvation of those relying on Him for their salvation. Mixed in with grace and mercy are references to merit, reward, works, and self-worth. As Rome explains it, by dying on the cross, Christ made entrance into heaven *possible*. For anyone to actually make it into heaven, however, he must be baptized, live a good life, and die in a proper state.

Consequently, when Catholics think about getting to heaven, what mainly goes through their minds is what *they* must do. Sometimes they don't include Jesus in their thinking at all. Of the 24 Catholics we interviewed outside Saint Patrick's Cathedral, asking them how they hoped to get into heaven, only three referred to Jesus. Only one Catholic made any meaningful reference to the cross.

When I told Father Warren, a particularly devout and loyal priest, about the results of our interviews, he objected. "I don't believe it," he said. "The Church teaches that salvation is through Christ. You can't earn your salvation. It is by the grace of God that we are saved. You might find some poorly taught Catholics who think otherwise, but that's not the teaching of the Church."

Admittedly, our sample group was small, but similar results have been found in talking to hundreds of Catholics around the world. The message that Catholics are getting from the Church is that their salvation is up to them. Christ has done His work; now they must do theirs.

Nevertheless, there is some merit to Father Warren's argument. In official Roman Catholic documents, all aspects of salvation are linked to Christ. At the same time, however, the Church teaches that no one can get to heaven solely by trusting Christ. Salvation is a joint effort. It's Him and you. In the words of the Church, Christ "unlocked the entrance to the heavenly kingdom, which the first man by his sin had locked against himself and all his posterity."[17] Unlocking the gates was Christ's part. Making it through those open gates by living a good life is man's part.

> By his death and Resurrection, Jesus Christ has "opened" heaven to us. . . . He makes partners in his heavenly glorification those who have believed in him

and remain faithful to his will—*Catechism of the Catholic Church.*[18]

What Father Warren said about Catholic salvation being by grace is also true, but only in a sense. Roman Catholicism teaches that an unbaptized person cannot earn the *initial* grace of justification. That grace is free, says the Church, being received through the sacrament of baptism. But once in the state of grace, Catholics can and must earn additional grace if they hope to make it to heaven.

Furthermore, what the Catholic Church calls grace is not grace at all. Roman Catholic grace is something that affixes to the soul. Catholics obtain it initially through baptism. It increases through reception of the Eucharist and other sacraments. Additional Catholic grace can be earned by performing good works. It can also be lost by committing a mortal sin, and regained through the sacrament of confession.

This, of course, is not biblical grace at all. Grace, as the Scriptures define it, is the undeserved favor of God toward sinners. It cannot be dispensed through rituals or earned by good works. Neither does God stop acting in grace toward His redeemed children who step out of line. Rather, He disciplines them in love (Hebrews 12:5-11).

Father Warren is also mistaken in saying that only a poorly instructed Catholic would forget to mention Jesus when asked how to get to heaven. Often it is the best-taught Catholics who are focusing on their works alone to get them to heaven. Father Miguel, a Roman Catholic priest whom we interviewed for the Spanish version of the video *Catholicism: Crisis of Faith*, comes to mind. We met him at the Shrine of Our Lady of Fatima in Portugal. He had led a group of pilgrims there from Spain to celebrate the feast of Mary's assumption. We asked him if he thought that he was going to heaven. "Of course!" he roared, gesturing with the upward swing of his arm and a big smile, amused at the thought of anyone asking a priest such a ridiculous question. "I've been a priest for

47 years!" That was all the answer he needed, at least in his mind.

Mother Teresa of Calcutta may also be confused about the grounds of salvation. She recently stated:

> One of the most demanding things for me is traveling everywhere—and with publicity. I have said to Jesus that if I don't go to heaven for anything else, I will be going to heaven for all the traveling with all the publicity, because it has purified me and sacrificed me and made me really ready to go to heaven.[19]

I would like to think that Mother Teresa was being facetious when she made those remarks, but her answer is typically Catholic. I fear that Mother Teresa, like many Catholics, is so wrapped up in personal works of righteousness that she doesn't realize that if she goes to heaven there will be only one reason: Jesus. Not her. Not Jesus plus her. But Jesus alone.

Catholics, however, are not trusting Jesus alone for their salvation. Week after week what they hear from the pulpit and through the liturgy is a gospel of works. The result is that Christ is not the center of their salvation—*they are*. It's not the poorly taught who believe this, but Catholics in general.

When I tried to explain this to Father Warren, he would have no part of it. I finally invited him to join me on the steps of his church the following Sunday. I suggested that we survey his parishioners—the Catholics that he had been teaching. We would determine together what they were trusting for their salvation and see how many of them mentioned the name of Jesus. Father Warren declined.

Brian was more daring. When he saw *Catholicism: Crisis of Faith,* he was convinced that the interviews outside Saint Patrick's Cathedral had been staged and that all the people were actors. He decided to run a test of his own at his parish, Saint Leander's Catholic Church in San Leandro, California. For the next several weeks as Sunday Mass let out, Brian asked the most devout

Catholics he could find how they hoped to get to heaven. Not one of the some 25 parishioners he spoke to even mentioned Jesus. All they talked about was loving God, loving their neighbor, and doing their best. Confused, Brian waited after Mass one Sunday and asked the parish priest how he hoped to get to heaven. When even the priest failed to mention the Lord Jesus, Brian realized that the Catholic Church had indeed gone astray. That was the last Sunday that either Brian or his wife, Ana, attended the Catholic Church.

You may want to conduct your own survey. Be careful, though, not to give away the answer in your question. For example, if you were to ask Catholics, "Do you believe that Jesus died on the cross for your sins?" expect all of them to answer yes. But if you ask, "How do you hope to get to heaven?" most Catholics will give you a list of activities that they must do. Only a small percentage will make any meaningful reference to Jesus or to His saving work on the cross. Fewer Catholics still, if any, will give the biblical answer: dependence upon Christ alone. The reason, of course, is that this is not what is taught in the Roman Catholic Church.

What exactly does the Church teach is the way of salvation? A popular post-Vatican II catechism provides the following summary of the Church's teaching:

> *Question:* What is necessary to be saved?
>
> *Answer:* You have to be brought into spiritual contact with that saving death of Jesus by faith and Baptism and loyal membership in His Church, by love of God and neighbor proved by obedience to His commandments, by the other Sacraments especially Holy Communion, by prayer and good works and by final perseverance, that is, preserving God's friendship and grace until death.[20]

Note the lack of emphasis on Jesus in this answer. The only mention of Him is with reference to being "brought into spiritual contact with that saving death of Jesus."

What the catechism means by this is that the person must have sanctifying grace in his soul. This, says the Church, unites a person to Jesus and gives him a participation in the divine life of God. According to the catechism, to obtain sanctifying grace and preserve it in one's soul, a Catholic must accomplish a list of ten requirements:

- believing
- being baptized
- being a loyal member of the Church
- loving God
- loving his neighbor
- keeping the Ten Commandments
- receiving the sacraments, especially Holy Communion
- praying
- doing good works
- dying in a state of grace

Based on this list, I have developed a technique for sharing the gospel with Catholics called the Pocket Evangelism Kit. It is made up of a number of illustrated cards, each representing one aspect of the Catholic plan of salvation. The cards are placed before the Catholic with a brief explanation of what each represents. The person is then asked to pick up those cards that he or she considers necessary for salvation. The purpose is to help the person see what he is trusting in for his salvation.

Catholics typically pick up several cards. A well-taught Catholic will take most, if not all of them, as the catechism answer previous instructs. Most Catholics make their selection with an attitude of "the more the better"!

Once the person has made his selection, he is asked several questions to help him rethink his selection. For example, should the person select the card titled "Keeping the Ten Commandments," he is asked, "Are you able to keep the Ten Commandments to God's standard?" If he picks the card titled "Loving Your Neighbor," he is asked, "Do you love your neighbor with the kind of love that God requires?" If he selects the "Doing Good Works" card, the question is, "How many good works do you have to do to get into heaven?" It is surprising how readily most Catholics admit that they can't do the things that they have selected as being necessary for salvation.

Should the Catholic pick up the card titled "Believing in God"—and most do—the person is asked, "What must you believe in order to go to heaven?" Here one would hope to hear something about the Lord Jesus and His saving work on the cross. More often than not, however, Catholics say nothing about Him. Instead they speak of the necessity of believing that God exists, that He is loving and merciful, or that He will forgive those who are truly sorry for their sins.

It is interesting to see the reaction of Catholics who fail to make any mention of Jesus when the omission is pointed out to them. Linda was such a person. I showed her the cards and asked her to pick up the ones that she thought were necessary for salvation. Linda chose most of them. When I asked her to explain her selection, she mentioned neither Jesus nor the cross. When I brought this omission to her attention, she became defensive.

"Your question was unfair!" Linda protested. "You asked what *I* had to do to be saved. If you had asked me about Jesus, I would have—" Linda suddenly paused and became reflective. She then continued in a quieter voice. "No, I have no excuse. I should have mentioned Jesus. I think I have just learned something very important."

I hoped that Linda had learned that no true Christian could forget to mention Jesus when asked how to get to heaven. I hoped that she realized that she needed to place her trust in Christ for salvation. But despite her admission, Linda continues to cling to the Roman Catholic Church and the false gospel that it teaches.

Knowing Where You're Going

When we asked Pat, a Catholic woman from Ohio whom we interviewed outside of Saint Patrick's Cathedral, how she hoped to get to heaven, she answered, "Catholicism isn't any different than any other religion. You obey the Ten Commandments, and I think you've got a pretty good chance. You can't go wrong with the Ten Commandments."

At least with regard to her first remark, Pat is correct. Catholicism isn't any different from most other religions. Whether it is Islam, Hinduism, a mixture of Chinese religions, or one of the Christian sects such as Mormonism or the Jehovah's Witnesses, most religions are basically the same. Like Roman Catholicism, they all teach that if you live a good life here on earth, you have a pretty good chance of enjoying blessing in the next life.

Biblical Christianity stands apart. It teaches that "no one is good except God alone" (Mark 10:18), that "all our righteous deeds are like a filthy garment" (Isaiah 64:6). True Christianity teaches that sinners can be accepted by God through the righteous work of another (Romans 3:21-26; 2 Corinthians 5:21). It proclaims a Savior who paid our penalty for us with His own life (Mark 10:45; 1 Peter 2:24). It tells of God's offer of eternal life to anyone who repents and believes (Mark 1:15; John 3:16; Ephesians 2:8-9). Those who accept this free gift of God can *know* that they are going to heaven, because their acceptance before God is in Christ, not in themselves. The Lord assured His disciples, saying, "Rejoice that your names are recorded in heaven" (Luke 10:20). He said, "I give eternal life to them, and they shall never perish; and no one shall snatch them out of My hand. My Father, who has given them to Me, is greater than all; and no one is able to snatch them out of the Father's hand" (John 10:28-29). The Holy Spirit also participates in guaranteeing the future of the redeemed. At the moment of salvation, the Spirit comes to dwell in each believer "as a pledge of our inheritance, with a view to the redemption of God's own possession, to the praise of His glory" (Ephesians 1:14).

Rash presumption is what Rome calls this. And right it would be if salvation were dependent, even in part, upon our own righteous deeds. Believing the promises of Scripture, however, is not presumption, but faith in God. It is doing what Jane DeLisi found so difficult the night we visited her, now some 16 years ago. It is allowing the Scriptures to speak for themselves, taking God at His word, and believing what He says.

Recently, I spoke with Jane. I asked her if she still has doubts about whether she will go to heaven or not.

"No," Jane answered without hesitation, "not since that night. I know that I believe in Jesus. I know that He died for me. I know that, if I died tonight, I would be in heaven. And that gives me great peace."

4

"My Children Are All Defecting"

Returning home from work one evening, Dave Sheridan had no idea that his life was about to be changed forever. His wife, Barbara, greeted him as usual with a smile and a kiss. Then came the first hint that something was up.

"Dave," Barbara began, "Kathleen wants to talk with you—alone."

Dave detected a nervous strain in Barbara's voice. Such a formal request from nine-year-old Kathleen, oldest of their three children, was also unusual. Realizing that the matter must be important, Dave asked Kathleen to join him in his den, offering her a seat in front of his desk.

"What do you want to talk about, Kathleen?" Dave asked.

"Daddy," she began, "I'm going to heaven."

Kathleen made the announcement so abruptly and with such confidence that Dave could only chuckle in amusement. He had never heard anyone claim such a thing. At the time he was the vice chairman of the parish council, head of a Catholic study group, and a trainer who prepared laity to serve as Eucharistic ministers and lectors. Dave also had helped formulate the baptism and first holy communion preparation programs for the parish. Still not feeling like he was doing enough, he began attending daily Mass. Yet despite all his learning, service, and participation in the sacraments, Dave didn't know if he was going to heaven.

She's just a kid, Dave thought to himself. *What does she know? I'll get to the bottom of this.*

"How do you know you're going to heaven, Kathleen?"

"Today I asked Jesus Christ to save me," Kathleen answered without hesitation.

"That's wonderful, dear," Dave replied, not really knowing what she was talking about. *I bet this is something they told her at that club the kids are attending*, he concluded.

It was the end of summer, and Barbara had run out of things for Kathleen and their other two small children to do. Finding an advertisement for a children's vacation Bible club, she had asked Dave if the kids could go. He hesitated when he learned that a Baptist church was sponsoring it. But figuring that no harm could be done and that it would be a way to keep the kids busy, he consented. Now two weeks later, he was wondering if he had made a mistake. *Ah, she's just a child*, he told himself.

A few days later, Barbara and the children attended the closing ceremony for the Vacation Bible School. There she met Bill Maupin, pastor of the sponsoring church. Bill asked Barbara if Kathleen had told her about her decision to trust Christ. When Barbara said that she had, Bill asked if he could visit her and her husband sometime to discuss Kathleen's decision. Barbara agreed, and they set up an appointment.

Dave was furious when he learned about the planned visit. "Absolutely not!" he told Barbara. Curious about what the pastor wanted to tell them, however, she kept putting off canceling the visit, hoping Dave would change his mind.

As the day of the visit approached, Dave found himself reconsidering. *What am I afraid of? I'm a well-educated Catholic and certainly know more about religion than any Baptist pastor.*

"Tell Bill to come on over," Dave finally told Barbara. "I'll be happy to talk to him."

When Bill arrived, Dave and Barbara welcomed him warmly, and the Sheridans prepared for what they thought would be a rousing discussion about religion. But Bill spoke only about the Lord and what He meant to him. The Sheridans had been around religious people all their lives. They had never, however, heard anyone talk about Jesus as Bill did. After the pastor had left, Dave commented to Barbara, "He talks as he if knows Jesus. He talks as if Jesus is still alive." Dave's image of Jesus was that of a dead man draped across the arms of Mary, as in Michelangelo's *Pieta*.

Bill began visiting the Sheridan home weekly to help Kathleen complete a workbook titled *What Jesus Wants You to Do*. Through those visits, a friendship developed between Bill and the Sheridan family, and after a time he invited Dave and Barbara to visit the church he pastored, Brecksville Chapel. Dave, however, turned him down. He wasn't interested, and besides, it was football season. Since Dave and his family were going to Saturday evening Mass to keep Sundays free for football, however, Dave told Barbara that if she and the kids wanted to visit Bill's church, it was fine with him.

The next Sunday, Barbara and her children visited Brecksville Chapel. They returned home excited about what they had found. The worship was simple and sincere, the Bible teaching understandable and practical. Barbara and the kids attended each of the next four weeks, each time returning home more enthusiastic than the time before.

When Dave finally decided that it was time to see for himself what was so special about this new church, his initial reaction was shock. Brecksville Chapel wasn't a church at all. It was nothing more than a room at the back of the Clippity Clop Saddle Shop on Route 82! Dave was accustomed to stained-glass sanctuaries and Gothic cathedrals. He couldn't imagine anyone worshiping in a saddle shop!

Regardless, even Dave could see that there was something special about the people there. The men especially impressed him. They prayed aloud in their own words and seemed to know the Bible almost as well as Bill. Dave also found the service interesting and informative.

Even though Dave liked Brecksville Chapel, as the weeks went by he felt increasingly uncomfortable with the direction that his family was heading. His fears were confirmed during one of Bill's visits to the Sheridan home a short time later. Colleen, the Sheridans' middle child, announced, "Daddy, I'd like to receive Jesus Christ as my personal Savior!"

Colleen was preparing to receive her first Holy Communion. Dave knew, however, that Colleen wasn't referring to receiving Christ at Mass. She was talking like a Baptist!

"She's only seven years old," Dave apologized to Bill. "I don't think she knows what she's asking."

Bill, however, took Colleen's request seriously. He asked her several questions and then carefully reviewed with Colleen the way of salvation. Though her parents couldn't completely follow Bill's explanation themselves, it was clear to them from Colleen's answers that she knew exactly what Bill was talking about. Finally, Bill asked Dave and Barbara if they had any objections to Colleen praying to receive Jesus Christ as her personal Savior. How could they say no?

Colleen and Bill got down on their knees, Dave and Barbara following them. Then Colleen told God that she was a sinner and wanted Jesus to save her.

What's happening? Dave thought to himself as his daughter prayed. *I've raised these children to be good Catholics. Now they're all defecting!*

A Betrayal of One's Religious Heritage

What should have been a reason for rejoicing, Dave Sheridan could only see as a cause of concern. As long as his wife and children continued to go to Mass with him on Saturdays, it was fine—though maybe a bit worrisome—for his family on Sundays to visit the Baptist church, to pray with Bill and his congregation, and even to learn from him about the Bible. Since the Second Vatican Council, the Roman Catholic Church has taught that all Christians are part of the family of God. Theology aside, however, for Dave there were only two kinds of Christians: Catholics and non-Catholics. And now with two of his children talking about God and salvation more like Baptists than Catholics, Dave felt that the Sheridan family had edged dangerously close to the line that divides.

Catholics consider their Church to be in a class by itself. It's *the* Church, the *Catholic* Church with a capital C. The rest of Christendom is to be respected, but remains, nevertheless, one step below. *Separated brethren*, as the Church calls them, are at best different. At worst, they are members of breakaway churches started by heretics and rebels.

The Catholic Church, on the other hand, is the true Church. It alone dates back to the beginning. As Catholics profess each week at Mass, it is the "one, holy, catholic, and apostolic church" instituted by Christ. Its bishops are the successors of Christ's 12 apostles. Its pope has inherited the throne of Saint Peter, to whom Christ said, "Thou art Peter; and upon this rock I will build my church" (Matthew 16:18, Douay Rheims Version). And although since the Second Vatican Council the Church has instructed its people to be more accepting of non-Catholic Christians, it has at the same time told them that in the Roman Catholic Church alone can be found the *fullness* of divinely revealed truth and means of salvation. Catholics proudly think of the Roman Catholic Church, now almost one billion people strong, as the biggest and the best. And should a family member dare to think of aligning himself or herself with anything less, the reaction can range anywhere from moderate concern to hostile opposition.

Consider the case of Theresa. When she told her Catholic parents, Bob and Margaret, that she had trusted Christ, their reaction was toward the concerned side of the scale. A freshman at the University of California, Berkeley, at the time, she arrived home late one night filled with excitement and joy. Waking her parents, she told, them, "Mom, Dad, I've got great news! I just accepted Christ as my Lord and Savior. I've just become a Christian."

"What do you mean you've just become a Christian?" her dad asked, irritated at such late-night nonsense.

"You've been a Christian all your life," added her mother. "What are you talking about?"

Theresa explained how Marc, her boyfriend and also a Catholic, and she had met earlier that evening with Rick, the leader of a college Bible club that Marc had been attending. Rick had explained to them the way of salvation. They both had then asked Jesus to come into their lives, trusting Him to save them.

"Everything was right out of the Bible," Theresa assured her parents.

That did little to lessen their fears. After some discussion, they all said good night, but sleep didn't come easily for any of them. Theresa, filled with excitement, lay awake reviewing the evening's events. Bob and Margaret quietly discussed their daughter's announcement between themselves. They concluded that whatever their daughter had gotten herself into, it was up to them to get her out. Hopefully it was only a passing interest that would soon fade.

In the weeks that followed, however, Theresa became increasingly involved in her newfound faith. She started reading the Bible each day and visiting a small Christian church in the neighborhood. She and Marc also started using their Friday evening date night to attend a home Bible study that Rick taught for college students.

"Theresa, you're taking this a little too far," her dad finally warned her. "It's one thing to go to church; it's another thing to let it consume your life. You're turning into a fanatic. I'm starting to get concerned about you."

Theresa tried to explain how important her commitment to Christ was to her and what she had learned from the Bible about salvation. But that only seemed to make things worse.

"Hell isn't real," her mom told her. "I just don't buy this stuff you're giving us."

"I sent you to Berkeley to broaden your mind," her dad complained, "and instead you're narrowing it. You don't believe the Creation story, do you? Do you really think that a whale swallowed Jonah?" he asked, looking at her like she was crazy.

"Theresa, you're really going off the deep end. We're beginning to think you and Marc have gotten involved in a cult," said her mother.

"You're going to become a nun," her brother began to tease.

Theresa shed a lot of tears in those days, mostly because her family whom she loved was heading to hell and refused to listen. It was an equally difficult time for her parents. Nevertheless, the trouble Theresa and her family experienced appears mild when compared to what some Catholics go through when a family member converts.

Take, for example, Pilar, a young woman living in Northern Spain. When she told her Catholic parents of her decision to be baptized at a small evangelical church, their reaction was one of hostile opposition. They gave Pilar an ultimatum: either stop associating with the evangelicals and their church or get out of the house. The next day, realizing that their daughter would not yield to their demands, they put Pilar and all her possessions out on the street. The young woman phoned a missionary couple who was helping to establish the church and asked them what she should do. They came and got her, welcoming her into their home. Pilar's parents retaliated by picketing the church each Sunday for over a year. They hurled abuses at all who entered and told everyone who passed by that the group was a cult that had kidnapped their daughter.

Another example is what happened to Renae. When she trusted Christ at age 20 and told her parents that she was leaving the Catholic Church, they also became angry, especially her father. First he disowned her, placing her photograph facedown on the living room mantel and cutting her picture out of a family portrait. When that didn't bring her back into the Church, he threatened to kill two of the elders of the evangelical church she had begun to attend.

Renae's boyfriend, Joe, experienced similar family troubles when he informed his parents that he was going to be baptized at the same church. His father told him, "You leave the Church, and, as far as I'm concerned, you no longer exist." After that Joe's father refused to talk to him or acknowledge his presence. When the father answered phone calls for Joe, he would drop the receiver and walk away without telling him. After six unbearable months, Joe decided he would have to move out.

Three years later, Joe and Renae married. By then her father had cooled down enough to attend the wedding. By the frown he wore to the ceremony, however, he made it clear that he did not approve. Joe's father refused to attend. He continued to ignore Joe, Renae, and even their children after they were born. On more than one occasion Joe's father walked away from his grandson, who with outstretched arms was seeking to be picked up by his grandfather. It took six years after Joe's conversion before his father finally began to soften.

The results were just as tragic when a Catholic man, an only son living with his elderly parents in rural Ireland, came to Christ. When he informed his parents of his decision to leave the Church, they warned him harshly and did everything in their power to persuade him to change his mind. The son held fast and in time won his father to the Lord through his godly behavior. The day after his father confessed faith in Christ, his mother donned a traditional widow's gown, black from head to toe. From that day onward, she refused to acknowledge the presence of either her husband or son, treating them both as if dead.

Why do some Catholics respond so strongly when one of their family members announces that he or she, in a desire to follow Christ, has chosen another church? Much of the reason has to do with Rome's exalted teachings about itself. The Church says that it, as the dispenser of the sacraments, is necessary for salvation. Vatican II stated that no one could be saved, who, "knowing that the Catholic Church was founded as necessary by God through Christ, would refuse either to enter it, or to remain in it."[21] Additionally, the Church says that the pope is the *vicar*, or representative, of Christ on earth. He is also the *pontiff*, high priest of the people of God. In view of these teachings, many Catholics equate God and the Church. To be loyal to God means to be loyal to the Church. To reject the Church is to reject God.

A Betrayal of One's Family Heritage

Often the reason that Catholics react so strongly when a family member converts has more to do with family and culture than it has to do with theology. Having been born Hispanic, or Italian, or Irish, or French, or Filipino, Polish, Austrian, or any one of the other predominately Catholic ethnic groups, Catholicism is "in their blood." It's part of their inherited culture. It shapes not only their beliefs about God, but also the way they see themselves and the world around them. An integral part of their personal and family identity, it's one of the "givens" by which they define themselves. And like one's last name, it's not something a person normally thinks about changing or may change without serious repercussions. In many Catholic strongholds, to leave the

Church and become a Protestant is considered a betrayal of one's family and culture.

Consider the heartbreak that parents must experience when a son or daughter announces that he or she has decided to leave the Catholic Church for an evangelical one. Parents feel that they have failed in the solemn responsibility of passing on spiritual values that have been handed down for centuries from one generation to the next. They should have done more, prayed more, sacrificed more. They can't help but take the decision personally. Coupled with this are the feelings of embarrassment and shame as news of the conversion travels through the parish and among the relatives. Finally, there is a sense of great loss and disappointment. On Sunday mornings the family will be divided, separating to worship at different and often opposing churches. The long-hoped-for wedding in the Catholic Church will never be. Neither will there be the family celebrations as grandchildren are baptized and later receive their first Holy Communion and confirmation. And as life comes to an end, there will be no Catholic funeral or burial in the family plot at the Catholic cemetery. The familiar milestones that have marked the passage of life for generations have been ripped up and carried off.

A Rejection, but Not of God, Family, or Culture

When a born-again Catholic chooses to leave the Church, others may interpret the decision as a rejection of God, family, and culture, but it is not. It is a rejection of Rome's false religious system. Having concluded from the Scriptures that the Roman Catholic Church is not the church founded by Christ, but rather an apostate form of Christianity, the new believer must leave. He cannot remain, without being disobedient to God, in an institution that teaches a false gospel. His decision is essentially the same as that of the first Christians who left apostate Judaism. Peter told the Jewish high priest, "We must obey God rather than men" (Acts 5:29).

Though the new Christian realizes that leaving the Catholic Church will hurt those closest to him, the decision to leave is not a rejection of family. To the contrary, it is only after a person has been born again and regenerated by the Holy Spirit that he can begin to love his family as he ought. As we shall see in the next chapter, the new believer feels the pain of leaving as keenly as does his family.

As the decision to leave the Church is not a rejection of family, neither is it a rejection of one's culture or ethnic heritage. Though Catholicism tends to intertwine itself into a culture, the two are not inseparable. One does not have to be Catholic to be Italian, Hispanic, or Filipino. Indeed, all traditionally Catholic countries now also have communities of non-Catholic Christians. This is especially true in Latin America, which now has as many regular church-attending Protestants as it does Catholics, though most nonchurchgoers still consider themselves Catholic.

It usually takes time—often several years—before Catholic family members can recover from the initial hurt of a member's conversion and see beyond it. Then, as the believer lives out his faith, family members begin to realize that, far from having rejected God, the convert is highly devoted to God and has an enviable relationship with God. They take notice as the person puts aside sinful and selfish ways and becomes increasingly Christlike in character. They come to see that, far from having rejected the family, the convert has become more loving, caring, and ready to serve. Only then is a Catholic family willing to reconsider what has happened and the possibility that there may have been matters of principle and truth involved in the convert's decision to leave the Church. Only then are they willing to consider the possibility that maybe the defector is right, that maybe they are the ones who are out of step with God.

That was the process that Tom and Franca went through when Gabriella, their 16-year-old daughter, announced that she had trusted Christ and wanted to be baptized. They knew that she had been going to a Bible study for high school and college students sponsored by an evangelical church. It concerned them that it wasn't Catholic, but when they saw an improvement in their daughter's sometimes-rebellious attitude, they decided to let her attend. When she said that she had been born again and wanted to be baptized, however, they felt they had made a mistake.

I later asked Tom and Franca how they felt when Gabriella first informed them of her decision.

"It disturbed me," Franca said, "because in my mind she was already baptized. If that was what was needed to get into heaven, she already had it. I could see no reason to have it done again. I was hurt. I felt that she was pulling away from us, that she no longer belonged to our spiritual family."

Tom, Gabriella's father, had a similar reaction. "I really felt lonely. I felt I didn't have any more importance in her life. I felt that she was leaving us for something else."

Terribly hurt and concerned that their daughter was getting involved with a cult, Tom and Franca forbade her to be baptized. Gabriella asked advice from the Christians at the Bible study where she had been attending, and they counseled her to wait to be baptized until she was older. During the next four years, she lived out her faith at home. When Gabriella finally decided that the time had come for her to obey the Lord by being baptized regardless of her parents' wishes, the situation had changed. Her example at home had won her parents over. They not only gave their consent, but also accepted an invitation to attend her baptism, bringing Gabriella's two grandmothers along with them. It was the turning point for the family.

"When Gabriella was baptized," Franca now recalls, "she gave a speech, explaining how she had come to the Lord and why she was taking this step. She confessed that she was a sinner, but that living her own way was in the past. From now on, she said, she wanted to dedicate her life to the Lord Jesus. She said that she was grateful to her parents for what they had told her about the Lord. She also explained how she had come to know the Lord with her own heart. I loved it!"

So did her father, Tom.

"Gabriella's baptism was one of the greatest days of my life," Tom now says. "I came to understand what it's all about. It's hard for me to explain how I felt that day. It was a joyous day. I learned that I wasn't losing a child; I was gaining her closer to me. I learned that God sent His Son for us. It was the beginning of my own coming to the Lord."

Not long after her baptism, Gabriella's parents began to study the Scriptures. Then her brother started attending the youth group at her new church. Two years later, all three trusted Christ, were baptized, and left the Catholic Church.

Something similar to what happened in Gabriella's household occurred in the family of Dave and Barbara Sheridan, only much more quickly. As soon as little Colleen had finished asking Christ to save her, Bill Maupin, the Baptist pastor, turned to Dave and Barbara and asked, "How about Mom and Dad?"

"We need time to think," Dave told Bill. "All this is pretty new to us. We need time and more information—a lot more information."

Bill suggested that they start reading the Bible. "What I say about salvation doesn't really matter," he explained. "What does the Bible say? That's the important question."

The next day Barbara purchased Bibles for Dave and herself. That evening when Dave came home from work, he took one of the Bibles into his den and started looking for the Gospel of John—the place where Bill had told them to start. Barbara took her Bible upstairs to the master bedroom, and also began reading John.

When Dave finally found John's Gospel, his eyes fell on a promise of the Lord Jesus: "If you abide in My word, then you are truly disciples of Mine; and you shall know the truth, and the truth shall make you free" (John 8:31-32).

Dave silently offered a prayer to God. *That's what I want, Lord. I want to know the truth.*

Dave turned to the beginning of John's Gospel and read until he came to one of the best-loved verses in the Bible: "For God so loved the world, that He gave His only begotten Son, that whoever believes in Him should not perish, but have eternal life" (John 3:16).

The profound simplicity of the verse grabbed Dave. He stopped, picked up his Bible, and went upstairs to show Barbara. To his astonishment, when he entered the room, she too had stopped at John 3:16.

"Do you realize that if this verse is true," Dave said to Barbara, "it contradicts everything we know and believe as Catholics?"

The weeks that followed were filled with the excitement of making a great discovery. What they were reading seemed so different, so wonderfully different. As Catholics they were accustomed to the idea that they had to earn their way into heaven. Now they were coming to see from John's Gospel, Galatians, and Romans that salvation is the free gift of God. On the cross, Jesus took their place, suffering for their sins. What they needed to do was put their faith in Him to save them.

Finally one evening, Dave and Barbara got down on their knees on either side of their bed. Speaking to God in prayer, they each placed their trust in Christ. They renounced dependence upon the Catholic Church, the sacraments, and their own good works to get them into heaven. The next day they took their children out of the Catholic school and informed the parish priest of their decision to leave the Church.

5

"I Love
My Parents"

Though there was much to be said, not a word was spoken as Lyne and her mother washed the Saturday-evening dishes. Just 17 years old, Lyne was in the process of making life-changing decisions—ones that both she and her parents realized might tear their happy family apart. Too fearful to talk about it, they worked on in troubled silence.

It all started with conversations between Errol, Lyne's boyfriend, and Paul, an acquaintance from Montreal. Paul had been studying Hinduism and other Eastern religions when someone had directed him to the Bible and salvation through Jesus Christ. Paul repented and believed. He told Errol, a longtime friend. Errol also believed and was born again. He told Lyne.

Lyne found the message harder to accept. She was interested when Errol explained from the Scriptures God's free offer of salvation. She also enjoyed talking with the Christians at two small evangelical churches that they visited in an adjoining town. But when Errol pointed out the differences between what the Bible was saying about salvation and what Lyne had been taught in religion classes in Catholic school, she became concerned. When he then began to criticize the Church, she became defensive.

Lyne and her family were Catholics, as was Errol, as was everyone in their village of 4000 situated in central Quebec province, Canada. Catholic missionaries from France—members of orders such as the Society of Jesus (the Jesuits), the Society of Priests of Saint Sulpice (the Sulpicians), and the Ursuline nuns—had helped settle the region in the seventeenth and eighteenth centuries. They established a Catholic colony governed by a three-man council, permanently reserving one seat for the Catholic bishop. Clergy oversaw all aspects of education, health care, and general welfare. The Jesuits owned much of the land, and laws were passed that banned Protestants from residency. Though the Church today no longer retains civil authority in the region, its influence is still strong. Eighty-six percent of the people in the province of Quebec are practicing Roman Catholics. It has by far the highest concentration of Catholics in either Canada or the United States.

Lyne and her family were not just average Catholics; they helped run the parish. Her father worked as the church sacristan (the custodian in charge of the vestments, sacred utensils, and the sacristy where the priests prepared before saying Mass). Her mother directed the church choir. Lyne sang in the choir, served on the parish liturgical committee, and frequently read the Scriptures during the Mass.

Consequently, when Errol became critical of the Church, Lyne's whole life was threatened. After three weeks of intense discussion and debate, the matter came to a head.

"You're destroying everything I believe, Errol," Lyne complained. "I'm Catholic. I'll never change!"

"Lyne, you can't remain a Catholic," Errol fought back. "Look, there's only one major city in the world built on seven hills: Rome. Revelation 17:9 says that the woman who represents false religion in the end times sits on seven hills. You've seen for yourself that the Catholic Church has lied to us; it taught us a false way of salvation. I won't remain a Catholic, and neither should you."

Lyne took the Bible and carefully read Revelation 17 for herself. As she did, it all fell together. "Errol, I don't know why, but I see it now. There's no other church this chapter could be talking about. I'll stop going." She then added, "But I can't bear to face my parents."

Lyne's parents were already on the alert. They knew that she and Errol were studying the Bible and had been talking to evangelicals. "Be careful, Lyne," they had warned her. "These new friends of Errol are dangerous. They'll brainwash you." But realizing that Lyne was almost an adult, they stopped short of forbidding her to talk with them.

During the next few days, Lyne said nothing to her parents about her decision to leave the Church. By Saturday evening, however, she knew that she could avoid the issue no longer. The next morning her parents would be expecting her to join them at Mass. Too afraid to speak to her parents directly, she decided to leave them a note on the kitchen table. It simply read: *I won't be going to church tomorrow. Lyne.*

The next morning, Lyne's mother found the note, but nevertheless called up the stairs toward her daughter's bedroom as she always did. "Lyne, are you getting up?"

"Sorry, Mother," Lyne answered. "I won't be going to church this morning."

That was all that was said. With none of the family willing to confront the matter head-on, an uneasy, quiet tension set in: Lyne trying to avoid the topic; her parents studying her every expression, trying to figure out what was going on.

That week passed too quickly for Lyne. Soon it was Saturday evening again, and looming over her once more was her parents' expectation that she be at Mass the next morning. As her mother and she washed the dinner dishes at the kitchen sink, Lyne prayed for courage to tell her parents about her decision to leave the Church. Just then the phone rang, and the truth came out under the worst possible circumstances.

"Hello," Lyne's mother said, answering the phone. After a short pause she added, "Oh, hello, Hélène. I'll get her for you."

Lyne's heart sank. Hélène was the woman in charge of organizing the readers for the Mass. *Oh, no!* Lyne thought to herself. *Not now!*

"It's for you, Lyne. It's Hélène Laval."

Lyne took the receiver from her mother and, trying to sound casual, greeted the caller. "Good evening, Mrs. Laval."

"Hello, Lyne. I was calling to see if you would read at the nine o'clock Mass."

"No, Mrs. Laval," answered Lyne. With her mother standing beside her and listening to her every word, Lyne didn't want to say anything more.

"So, you can read at the 11 o'clock Mass?"

"No, Mrs. Laval."

"Well, then at the five o'clock?"

"No, Mrs. Laval."

"No? What do you mean? Lyne, you've always been willing to read before."

Lyne tried to find a way of escape, but realizing it was hopeless, finally blurted out, "I won't be going to Mass anymore."

"Oh!" answered the woman, too astonished to say anything else.

"Good-bye, Mrs. Laval," said Lyne, putting down the receiver.

"Lyne, do you realize what you're doing?" her mother asked, her voice trembling with emotion.

"Yes, Mother," Lyne answered. She knew all too well what she was doing and that there was no way to soften the blow for her mother. She could only watch as her mother broke down in deep sobbing and then retreated to her bedroom in tears. As she did, Lyne picked up her

Bible and went out to the front porch. Sitting on the top step of the stairs leading to the house, she began to pray.

Lord, this can't be right. Surely this isn't what You want! It's so hard. I love my parents too much to hurt them like this. I'm willing to do whatever You want, but I'm so confused. Help me, Lord.

Not knowing where to turn, Lyne opened her Bible. The first passage that her eyes fell on were words of the Lord Jesus. They came to her as counsel from heaven: "Everyone who has left houses or brothers or sisters or father or mother or children or farms for My name's sake, shall receive many times as much, and shall inherit eternal life" (Matthew 19:29).

Though the months ahead were difficult, Lyne never returned to the Catholic Church or again doubted the Lord's direction. The God of the universe had looked down from heaven, had seen a young French-Canadian woman trying to obey Him and, from the more than 30,000 verses of the Bible, had selected the very one that she needed to read.

Saved but Planning to Stay

In the previous chapter we looked at how Catholic families react when one of their members decides to leave the Church. Here we will consider the other side of the equation: what the born-again Catholic must face. The process starts with salvation and the realization that the Catholic Church is wrong. Unlike Lyne, however, most born-again Catholics do not immediately see leaving as a necessary consequence of believing.

Harry comes to mind. A muscular man with a bent toward hard drinking and fighting, Harry couldn't keep out of trouble. Having found the advice that his parish priest had been giving him ineffective, Harry decided to look elsewhere for help. The next Sunday he showed up at the evangelical church in his neighborhood. With his left arm in a cast, mending a break from his last brawl,

Harry explained his problem to Mike, one of the church elders.

Mike took Harry under his care and began sharing with him the way of salvation from the Scriptures. A few days later, Harry professed faith in Christ.

The results were immediately visible. Harry's aggressive nature transformed into zeal for God. In his mind, however, Harry was still a Catholic. And so, having found the help for which he had been looking, Harry said good-bye. He was going home to the Catholic Church.

"How many years have you been in the Catholic Church, Harry?" Mike asked him.

"Twenty-eight," Harry answered.

"How long have you known the Lord?"

"Two weeks."

"Does that tell you anything, Harry?"

Harry got the point. Why return to a Church that hadn't been able to help him or introduce him to the Lord?

Other born-again Catholics don't see this as readily. Challenged to leave the Church, they instinctively answer, "I was born Catholic, and I'll die Catholic."

"Don't tell me you were born a Catholic," one Filipino Christian is quick to correct his countrymen. "You were *born* a sinner; you were *baptized* a Catholic. It doesn't make any sense to give your dying allegiance to a religion simply because your family belongs to it. Had you been born in the southern region of the Philippines," he reminds them, "in all likelihood you would have been born a Muslim, not a Catholic. Would that make Islam the right religion for you?"

Still other Catholics, driven by misguided loyalties, remain in the Catholic Church, convinced that, despite its faults, it's Christ's church. They know that the Church doesn't preach the gospel, that the Mass is not what the Church says it is, and that a priest cannot absolve sins. Nevertheless, they remain, thinking that Christ is there.

But Christ is not there. He is not in the Eucharist. He is not in the tabernacle of the main altar. He is not hanging on the life-size crucifix suspended by cables over the priest's head. Christ does not dwell in buildings, but in the hearts of the redeemed. And where the gospel is not preached, the people remain dead in their sins, void of the life of God.

"Why do you seek the living One among the dead?" (Luke 24:5), the angel asked the women looking for the Lord in a graveyard on the morning of His resurrection. The same question might be asked of these born-again Catholics looking for the Lord Jesus in the Catholic Church. "He is not here, but He has risen!" (Luke 24:6), the angel told the women. These Catholics need to realize that the same is true of the Church of Rome. Christ is not there.

Staying in Hope of Changing the Church

Despite the miraculous circumstances under which Lyne found Matthew 19:29, some would say that she made a terrible mistake, that all the family friction was unnecessary. "Work within the system," they advise. "Share with others what you have found. If everyone leaves, how is the Catholic Church ever going to change?"

Such advice is both misinformed and unbiblical. Born-again Catholics staying within the Church are not going to change it. Rome's history over the past 500 years shows that it is moving away from the truth, not toward it. When in the sixteenth century several of the Church's theologians and priests called for reform, the Church responded with the sword and the stake. At the Council of Trent (1545–63), Rome's bishops turned errors into unchangeable dogmas, and pronounced solemn judgment upon anyone who taught otherwise. Most significantly, Trent formally rejected the doctrine of salvation through faith in Christ alone. [22] Since then the Church has been steadily moving further from the truth. In 1870, 533 Roman Catholic bishops proclaimed that the pope was infallible, immune to error in his official teaching. This placed the words of a man on the same level as the words of God in inspired Scripture. In 1854 the Vatican formally declared the doctrine of Mary's immaculate conception and in 1950 her assumption into heaven. These two doctrines fueled the modern Marian movement in which many Catholics have come to regard Mary almost as a goddess. Catholicism is getting worse, not better.

Some point to the Second Vatican Council (1962–65) and the Catholic charismatic renewal that began in 1967 as evidence that the Church is changing for the better. They claim that over the past 40 years the Catholic Church has become increasingly evangelical in its outlook.

But what has really changed? The goal of Vatican II was to update the Church, not to reform it. The Council modernized some practices; refocused the goals of the clergy and laity; refreshed the liturgy, making room for the language of the people to replace Latin at the Mass; and formally expressed the Church's new openness toward both other Christians and non-Christians. Vatican II did not change a single dogma of Roman Catholicism. To the contrary, the Second Vatican Council reemphasized the Church's traditional teachings, repeatedly citing in its documents the teaching of the previous 20 councils, and stating, "This sacred council accepts loyally the venerable faith our ancestors. . . . It proposes again the decrees of the Second Council of Nicea, of the Council of Florence, and of the Council of Trent."[23]

In 1994 the Catholic Church again restated in the *Catechism of the Catholic Church* its commitment to the traditional teachings of Roman Catholicism. The *Catechism*, the Church's first official summary of the faith in some 400 years, cited the Council of Trent 100 times.

While Vatican II did nothing to bring the Catholic Church back to biblical Christianity, some good did come out of the Catholic charismatic renewal, as the large numbers of born-again former Catholics now in evangelical churches attest. In its early days in the late sixties, the renewal was largely a lay movement. As Catholics began to seek God and read the Scriptures, the renewal spread quickly through the Catholic Church.

The experience of former priest Bob Bush, a Jesuit serving in California at the time, is typical of the era. He began a charismatic prayer meeting at the high school where he taught in 1970. It quickly grew to over 1000 people and had to move to a larger facility. "When it began," Bob told me recently, "people were hungry for God. The focus was on prayer directly to God and the reading of Scripture. Many people were touched by God and by the power of His Word."

That all changed by the late 1970s. Bishops began to issue directives that brought the movement firmly under Church control. They assigned liaisons to each group to keep watch and help guarantee Catholic orthodoxy. Teaching from Church-authorized books began to replace the Scriptures. Clergy became more visible at the meetings, and the praying of the Rosary prominent. Devotion to Mary and the celebration of the Mass became the focus.

"What happened," Bob Bush recounts, "was that everything got watered down and compromised. There was no longer any power in the movement. People stopped hearing from the Holy Spirit. They weren't having the radical changes in their lives as before. The Renewal became just another form of Catholicism." A more traditional priest was assigned to lead Bob's prayer group in 1978. Within a few years, it had dwindled down to nothing. Bob left the Church a short time later.

The recent emergence of an evangelical-looking form of Catholicism in certain countries is presently spawning new claims that Rome is becoming more biblical. But once again the change is only external. As will be discussed later in this book, the new look is nothing more than old-time Catholicism repackaged to capitalize on the success of the modern evangelical movement.

Others think that Rome must be changing because they have heard of a particular parish where the priest, supposedly having been born again, is preaching the gospel each week at Mass. I have never, however, been able to verify such a case. Occasionally a priest does get saved, but he will not be wearing a Roman collar for long if he starts preaching the gospel, refuses to perform the Sacrifice of the Mass, stops leading prayers to Mary, and ceases to hear confession. Even if a number of such born-again priests could be found, with more than 400,000 Roman Catholic priests in the world, what 10, 20, or even 100 priests do would hardly be a trend. The opposition that these men would be sure to experience from the Church would be a better indicator of the true course on which Rome is heading.

The Roman Catholic Church has not changed and it is not about to change. Consequently, counseling a newly born-again Catholic to remain within the system and make a difference is foolish. Practically speaking, what's the person supposed to do? Talk to a few of his friends? Go see the priest? Write a letter to Rome? Do such things really have the potential of reforming the Church?

The truth is that neither priests nor parishioners have any significant say in the direction of the Church. The Roman Catholic Church is not a democracy, but a hierarchical monarchy. Bishops, some 3250 in number, lead it. The seat of power is the Vatican. From there the pope rules as the supposed vicar of Christ and head of the bishops. Aiding the pope are his top advisers and administrators, known as *cardinals*. These oversee the *Roman Curia*—the powerful administrative and judicial offices of the Vatican.

This structure leaves no room for democratic change or for a grass-roots coalition seizing power. It is a top-down organization. The most the average Catholic can hope to do is influence the thinking of the hierarchy through means such as letters, petitions, and protest. None of these are encouraged or welcomed by the Church.

Even if a significant mechanism for popular change existed, think for a moment what would have to change in order for the Roman Catholic Church to become a biblical church. The pope would have to resign, acknowledging that Christ is the head of the church (Colossians 1:18). The bishops would have to drop their claim to sole teaching authority, recognizing the Holy Spirit as the church's only infallible and authoritative teacher (John 14:26; 16:13; 1 John 2:27). The Catholic priesthood would have to disband, confessing that the Sacrifice of the Mass is an insult to the finished work of Christ and that no one can forgive sin but God alone (Mark 2:7; Hebrews 10:18). Altars would need to be torn down, confession booths removed, statues destroyed (Exodus 20:4). Veneration and prayer to Mary and the saints would have to stop, so that Catholics might know that there is "one mediator also between God and men, the man Christ Jesus" (1 Timothy 2:5). The Church would have to confess that it has been preaching a false gospel, leading countless millions down the wide path that leads to destruction. It would have to acknowledge that baptism is not the instrument of justification, that its sacraments cannot dispense the grace of God, that eternal life is not a merited reward, and that venial sin, acts of penance, purgatory, and indulgences are all the inventions of men. Finally, the Church would have to begin proclaiming salvation by grace alone through faith alone in Christ alone and, forsaking all dependence upon Tradition, begin using the Scriptures alone as its guide to truth.

Clearly, there is no indication that any of this is likely to happen. Neither should we expect God to step in at this late date and revamp the Church of Rome. God is in the business of saving people, not restructuring man-made institutions such as the Roman Catholic Church.

God's instruction to those who find themselves in apostate churches teaching a false gospel is to get out: "Come out of her, my people, that you may not participate in her sins and that you may not receive of her plagues; for her sins have piled up as high as heaven, and God has remembered her iniquities" (Revelation 18:4-5).

For anyone, therefore, to advise a born-again Catholic to remain in the Church and try to change it is to exhibit an appalling lack of understanding of the commands of God, the nature of the Roman Catholic Church, and the needs of a new believer. Newly born-again Christians need nurturing and the "pure milk of the word" (1 Peter 2:2), not the half-truths, lies, and confusion of Roman Catholicism. They need the fellowship of like-minded believers. They need to be part of a church in which they can worship God, free of idolatry and false sacrifice.

Staying in Hope of Reaching Family

Some born-again Catholics, knowing the Catholic Church to be both wrong and impossible to reform, remain nevertheless, hoping to reach unsaved Catholic family and friends with the gospel. They believe that if they leave the Church, their family will cut them off and their opportunity to influence them will be lost. But actually the opposite is true. Leaving makes the clearest and strongest statement to family and friends. It is as we separate ourselves from false religion that the difference between truth and error becomes apparent. This provides the greatest opportunity of reaching one's family with the gospel.

Time and again this has proven to be the case. As recounted in the previous chapter, it was through the clear confessions of their two daughters, Kathleen and Colleen, that Dave and Barbara Sheridan came to Christ. A short time later their son also was born again. In a similar way, God used Gabriella's example at home and her baptism to bring her family to the Lord. Though Theresa, also mentioned in the previous chapter, at first experienced opposition from her family, one by one she saw her parents, her sister, and two brothers saved. Marc, her boyfriend, was used by God to see his two brothers, three sisters, and father come to Christ in quick succession.

Lyne, whose story is told at the beginning of this chapter, has seen her two brothers come to Christ. Harry, also mentioned earlier in this chapter, never did go back to the Catholic Church. Instead his family came to him, visiting his new church in a steady stream. Several made professions of faith.

Trying to witness to family and friends from within the Church only confuses the issues. It sends mixed signals. With his lips the born-again Catholic may be trying to explain biblical salvation to those around him, but with his life he is telling them that his beliefs are basically compatible with Roman Catholicism. Should he become openly critical of the Church, his fellow Catholics might rightly ask him, "If the Church is so wrong, what are you doing here?"

The Scriptures call us to separate ourselves from false religion:

> Do not be bound together with unbelievers; for what partnership have righteousness and lawlessness, or what fellowship has light with darkness? Or what harmony has Christ with Belial, or what has a believer in common with an unbeliever? Or what agreement has the temple of God with idols? For we are the temple of the living God; just as God said,
>
>> "I will dwell in them and walk among them;
>> And I will be their God, and they shall be My people.
>> Therefore, come out from their midst and be separate," says the Lord.
>> "And do not touch what is unclean" (2 Corinthians 6:14-17).

The Lord makes the following promises to those who obey:

> "And I will welcome you.
> And I will be a father to you,
> And you shall be sons and daughters to Me,"
> Says the Lord Almighty (2 Corinthians 6:17-18).

Family and friends may become angry and critical, but that is part of the cost of being Christ's disciple. The Lord Jesus warned those who would follow Him to expect family troubles:

Do not think that I came to bring peace on the earth; I did not come to bring peace, but a sword. For I came to set a man against his father, and a daughter against her mother, and a daughter-in-law against her mother-in-law; and a man's enemies will be the members of his household (Matthew 10:34-36).

It has never been popular to follow Jesus. Many of the first believers were martyred for their faith. The same is true of hundreds of thousands of believers who, during the time of the Reformation, paid with their lives for refusing to submit to Rome.

The Lord Himself was rejected by both His family and His people, being crucified outside of Jerusalem in the company of criminals. He did this for us. God now exhorts us to "go out to Him outside the camp, bearing His reproach" (Hebrews 13:13). This means placing loyalty to Christ above that to family, ethnicity, country, and church. Jesus taught: "He who loves father or mother more than Me is not worthy of Me; and he who loves son or daughter more than Me is not worthy of Me" (Matthew 10:37).

Though putting Christ first does not mean turning one's back on family and friends, as some may think, it may mean facing some difficult questions. The following letter, received from a young Catholic woman on the verge of leaving the Church, illustrates the kinds of issues a born-again Catholic must resolve.

Dear Mr. McCarthy,

I am an eighteen-year-old senior in high school and I am now in the process of reading your book, *The Gospel According to Rome*. I was confirmed into the Catholic Church early last summer. I now wish that I had given it more thought. I wish that I had known what I know now about what the Catholic Church stands for and believes in. I wish I had read your book earlier.

While I was going through confirmation class, the teachers stressed that we needed to be sure that we would continue to follow and be part of the Church before we were confirmed. At the time I trusted completely in the Church and thought I would spend the rest of my life as a member of it. I now realize that it was blind faith. When non-Catholic friends and acquaintances would argue with me about the Church, I would always defend it.

A few months ago a very good friend of mine made a point about the Church that I couldn't defend. That was the first thing said to me against the Catholic Church that I could not argue. This point bothered me for several weeks until I finally asked the director of religious education at my church about it. I have always been very close to her and she gave me an answer that sounded reasonable. She also gave me a book containing the Second Vatican Council documents. I started reading it that very night, thinking that it would make me, once again, confident in my faith in the Church. It did the very opposite.

As I read, I started to realize how ridiculous most of it was. The Catholic Church has a rule for everything. I also noticed that the book was larger than the Bible. Isn't Christianity following what the Bible says? But Catholics must follow what the Church says. Through this time I have also been talking with my friend. He is a person that I trust a lot and also whose opinion I value. He is a member of a local Bible church which fellow students in my religious education class have cruelly nicknamed "The Psycho Bible Barn." I don't see the humor in it, and don't see how a church that follows the Bible could be "psycho." Also, leaders in my church like to talk about other churches of its kind as if what they do and believe is wrong, all the while believing they are being ecumenically correct by referring to them as "fundamentalist" churches.

I know that I cannot continue being a member of the Roman Catholic Church, but I am very scared of the results. My family is mostly all Catholic and would be shocked if they knew what I am contemplating. How does one leave the Church? Is it a formal termination or do I just stop going to Mass? Will I be excommunicated? How did your family react when you left the Church?

Sincerely,

Marnie

Marnie asks three good questions—ones that every born-again Catholic who has ever contemplated leaving the Church must face at one time or another.

How does one leave the Church? Is it a formal termination or do I just stop going to Mass?

Probably the best way for a born-again Catholic to leave is to visit the parish priest and inform him of the decision. This also provides an opportunity to share the gospel with him—a responsibility that should not be overlooked. If the new believer does not feel strong enough to speak to the priest alone, he should take with him someone who knows the Bible well and will be able to answer objections.

Most born-again Catholics, however, just stop going, not wanting to cause a fuss. With the pastoral staff of many parishes already overburdened, it is unlikely that one person leaving will even be missed. It is not unusual for a parish of over 2000 people to have only one priest. In some places there are so few priests that two or three parishes share a single priest. Four years after my wife and I left the Catholic Church, we were still receiving in the mail envelopes for our Easter offering from our last parish.

Will I be excommunicated?

I am not aware in modern times of the Church explicitly excommunicating a regular lay Catholic. Occasionally, the Vatican will formally declare a priest or lay theologian excommunicated. The most recent case was Oblate Father Tissa Balasuriya, 72, of Sri Lanka. An outspoken theologian, he held to a number of beliefs at odds with Rome. Among other things, Balasuriya disputed the Church's teaching on papal authority—one offense that the Vatican will not tolerate. After four years of warnings, the Vatican said that Father Balasuriya had essentially excommunicated himself by his refusal to submit to Rome. Church law states that "an apostate from the faith, a heretic or a schismatic incurs automatic excommunication."[24] Accordingly, in the eyes of the Church, every former Catholic who has openly repudiated Roman Catholicism as unbiblical has been automatically excommunicated.

How did your family react when you left the Church?

As we saw in the previous chapter, Catholic families usually take it pretty hard when a member announces that he or she is leaving the Church. Nevertheless, as we have also seen, obeying the Lord is the best thing for everyone involved.

When I told my parents that I was leaving the Catholic Church, they became very upset. They were immigrants from Ireland, and Catholicism was all they knew. To have their eldest son reject the faith was a terrible disappointment to them. I told them across the kitchen table during a visit to their home, explaining as gently as I knew how why I could no longer remain a Catholic. My dad lost his temper and stormed out of the house in a rage. He refused to return until I had left. My mother broke down in tears. I was the first in the clan to reject Roman Catholicism. It created considerable grief for the entire family.

My dad remained upset with me for many years, including a three-year stretch during which he refused to see me or talk to me. At length, however, we were reconciled. In the final months of his life, I was able to speak to him about the Lord and the way of salvation on several occasions. As far as I know, however, he never openly professed faith in Christ alone for salvation.

My mom passed away several years before my dad. When I first trusted Christ, she and I had several good discussions about the Lord and the way of salvation. These talks became more strained, however, after I left the Catholic Church. Eventually she refused to talk about spiritual things with me altogether. A few years later she developed cancer, her health quickly declined, and she became confined to a hospital bed at home. One day about two months before she died, Jean and three of my sisters were sitting beside her bed when my mom made a startling announcement.

"You know, girls," my mother began, "Jean and I have our differences about what we believe. But what's most important is that we both believe that Jesus Christ died for our sins, and that He was buried, and that He rose again."

Jean immediately recognized the significance of my mom's announcement. In a family that had been torn apart by the gospel, my mother, who had always been the spiritual mainstay of the family, was saying she was in basic agreement with Jean and me. Additionally, in her listing of what was "most important," there was no mention of good works, receiving the sacraments, or going to Mass—all essential elements of salvation according to the Catholic Church.

I was in another room at the time, and when Jean came and told me what my mother had said, I was surprised but only cautiously optimistic. All Catholics believe, at least intellectually, that Jesus died for our sins, was buried, and rose on the third day. But that doesn't mean that they are trusting Him for salvation.

"You ought to go talk to Mom about it, Jim," Jean encouraged. "She sounded different."

I was hesitant; the subject had been taboo for so long. But at Jean's prompting, I started looking for an opportunity to talk to my mom alone. When it came, I found her open and wanting to talk about the Lord once more. She was fairly weak by then, however, and lengthy discussion was impossible. I went away encouraged, but still unsure as to whether she was actually saved.

A few days later, Jean and I had another opportunity to speak with my mother. She asked us to encourage my brothers and sisters to read the Scriptures. She also requested a supply of Bibles so that she could give them to her children and other friends and relatives. A list of two dozen names was drawn up, and Mom dictated short inscriptions to be placed in each Bible.

With each passing day, it was becoming more evident that my mother had had a spiritual awakening. What I didn't know at the time—only learning it after my mom's death while arranging some of her things—was that she had become a quiet student of the Bible. During the years that she had refused to talk to me about the Lord, I had continued to give her short books, simple courses, and audiotapes about the Bible. My mom had received these politely but without comment, not wanting to get into another religious discussion. Unknown to me, however, she was carefully reading everything I gave her, underlining important passages, and even completing a correspondence course called *What the Bible Teaches*. She wrote summaries of portions of the Scriptures and had marked important passages in her Bible. I was unaware of any of this until after her death. So even after my mother asked us to buy her the Bibles, I still wasn't sure that she had been born again. I needed more proof.

As Mom's health continued to decline, family members began to drop by for one last visit. One was a Catholic priest, a cousin of hers. She asked him, "Father, if we're forgiven our sins because of the cross, why do we have to confess them in the sacrament of penance?"

I was astounded. Was my mother really saved? Had she come to understand the biblical way of salvation? Was she finally beginning to see the contradictions within Roman Catholicism?

About that time I received the confirmation for which I had been looking. We learned that a short time earlier my mom had written out a prayer that she wanted my dad to read and keep before him. Though very weak at the time, she got out of bed and taped it to his shaving mirror. When I read the prayer, I knew that her faith was in Christ alone to save her. It read:

Lord Jesus! I need You. Thank You for dying on the cross for my sins. I open the door of my life and receive You as my Savior and Lord. Thank You for forgiving my sins. Take control of my life. Make me the kind of person You want me to be.

She went to be with her Lord a few days later.

6

"You'll Never Leave"

As the young priest opened the rectory door, Wilma Sullivan blurted out her request: "Father Phil, I need to talk to you."

"Wilma, I'm awfully busy right now," answered the priest, trying to excuse himself. Father Phil knew her well. Wilma was an ex-nun, having spent four years with the Sisters of Mercy. She attended his church and sang in the choir that he directed. He also knew that the young woman could be talkative.

"You've got to talk to me, Father," Wilma pleaded. She paused long enough to gather her thoughts, and then continued, carefully choosing each word. "I'm trying to salvage everything I've believed for 29 years as a Catholic." With urgency in her voice, she added, "Please talk to me."

The priest knew he couldn't refuse her. "Come on in, Wilma," he finally said, swinging the door open.

Wilma followed the priest through the entry hall into a counseling room. It was arranged much like a small office. He showed her to a seat in front of a desk and excused himself to notify his housekeeper of the change in his schedule.

"Now, what's this all about, Wilma?" Father Phil asked, reentering the room.

As the priest took a seat across the desk from her, Wilma noticed that he was eyeing the Bible that she had brought with her, now resting in her lap. It made her feel somewhat uncomfortable, but that didn't matter now.

"Father, my life is in turmoil," Wilma began in a slow, steady voice. "I need some answers."

"I'll do what I can. What's the problem?"

"I'm having terrible doubts."

"About what?"

"Everything! I'm not sure where to begin."

"When did they start?"

"A little over two weeks ago. I was in the hospital awaiting surgery. One evening a patient from across the hall visited me. Her name was Lenore. She had heard that I was an ex-nun and wanted to meet me. After some friendly conversation, Lenore asked me whether I had any doubts about going to heaven if I died during surgery."

"That was a rather brash question," Father Phil interjected. "Some people are absolutely tactless."

"The nurses thought so too," Wilma added. "They shooed Lenore away, afraid that she was going to upset me. But you know, Father, I think it was a good question. I could see that Lenore was genuinely concerned for me, and it made me think, *What would happen to me if I died?*

"After we both got out of the hospital, Lenore and I got together and talked some more, mostly about religion. I enjoyed the conversation until some of her questions started challenging my beliefs as a Catholic. I finally said, 'Listen, Lenore, I'm a Catholic, and I'm satisfied with my religion.'"

"Good for you, Wilma!" Father Phil applauded. "None of this surprises me. I've heard it all before."

"I did admit to her, though, that I had one question about my faith."

"And what's that?"

"I told her about something that happened while I was still in the convent. I was at Mass, kneeling at the altar rail about to receive communion. The priest came up to me, held the host in front of me, and said, 'The body of Christ.' I knew I was supposed to say, 'Amen,' but I found myself doubting. I was thinking to myself, *Is it really? Is that small bread wafer really Christ?"*

"Wilma, I don't know if you should have told her that. We all experience doubts. That's only natural. You shouldn't let it bother you."

"But that doubt has stayed with me. And that's not all, Father Phil. Lenore began showing me passages from the Bible. For example—" Wilma shifted the Bible in her lap and lifted it onto the desk. It was stuffed with book markers. After checking several locations, she opened it to the Book of Hebrews, chapter 10.

"Father Phil, the Bible says that 'we have been sanctified by the offering of the body of Jesus Christ once for all.' A few verses later it says, 'Now where there is forgiveness of these things, there is no longer any offering for sin.'"

"I'm aware of those verses."

"I'm sure I must have read them before also, Father. But when Lenore showed them to me, I saw something I hadn't seen before. She asked me whether I believed that the Bible was God's Word. I told her that I did. She then said, 'How many times does God say in the Bible that Jesus had to be offered for sin?' I told her we had just read it: 'once for all.' I said, 'Lenore, what's wrong with that?' She answered, 'How many times does your Church offer Christ for sin?' Father Phil, I was about to say, 'Every day at every Mass,' when it struck me that that contradicted the Bible. I didn't know what to say. I just looked at her with my mouth open."

"She was trying to confuse you, Wilma. I've run into people like her before. Don't pay any attention to them."

"Lenore said, 'Wilma, they're different, aren't they? What your Church says and what the Bible says.' I didn't know how to answer her. Then she said to me, 'So who are you going to trust? God who cannot lie to you in the Bible, or men who can make mistakes?' Father Phil, that was only the beginning."

For the next 45 minutes, Wilma recounted how Lenore and she had met almost daily over the past two weeks, studying the Bible and talking about what it said. Wilma had also visited Lenore's church and met her pastor. She reviewed with Father Phil their discussions on worship, devotion to Mary, the sacraments, purgatory, baptism, and the way of salvation. The priest listened without comment or objection. Wilma, on the other hand, became more impassioned with each new topic.

"Father Phil," Wilma told the priest, "what Lenore was showing me from the Bible made a lot of sense. I found the Bible, my *Catholic Bible* saying one thing and the Church saying something else. Father Phil, the Bible says—"

"I don't care what the Bible says," the priest finally interrupted. "The Church doesn't depend just on what the Bible says for her doctrine. We have Tradition. You of all people, Wilma, should know that. If your reading of the Bible doesn't line up with the Church's teaching, you know what you need to do: Put your Bible down and do what the Church tells you to do. That's why we have the Church."

"But Father Phil, these matters are substantial. I can't just ignore the Scriptures," Wilma answered, now more agitated than ever. She paused long enough to calm herself, and then added, "I'm thinking of leaving the Church."

"Wilma, you'll never leave the Catholic Church."

"I've been here for almost an hour. You have no answers for my questions. How can you tell me that I'll never leave?"

"Wilma, you're too steeped in the Tradition of the Church. You'll never leave. Never!"

Bound to the Church

Generally speaking, Father Phil was right. Most Catholics will never leave the Church. They may have their doubts. Their attendance at weekly Mass may become sporadic. They may be—and frequently are— critical of their pope, bishops, and priests. They often disagree with the Church's moral teachings. They may wander, sampling other -ologies and -isms. They may even incorporate aspects of other belief systems into their faith. But leave the Catholic Church? Never. Even today with all its changes, the axiom still stands: *Once a Catholic, always a Catholic.*

Relatively few Catholics even *think* of leaving. In 1987 pollsters measured the loyalty of the American membership of the Roman Catholic Church. Only 6 percent of the Catholics they interviewed said that they were seriously thinking of leaving the Church. Only 2 percent said that it was likely that they would go. In a culture as open to change as that of the United States, these results were unexpected.

Why are Catholics so loyal? Of the many factors binding Catholics to the Church, one of the most powerful is the Mass. The Second Vatican Council described the Mass as "the source and summit of the whole Christian life,"[25] "the greatest gift of all."[26] It is the focal point of Catholic liturgy around which everything else revolves. The Mass is the primary point of contact between Catholics and the Church, and the chief way that the Catholic faith is handed down from one generation to the next.

The Church mandates that all Catholics attend Mass weekly. It recognizes some reasons for failure to meet this "holy obligation," such as illness, caring for a sick child or parent, or the inability to get to church while traveling. But deliberate disobedience is a mortal sin. To be forgiven, a Catholic must confess how many times he missed Mass to a priest during the sacrament of penance.

The Church teaches that Catholics are not only morally obliged to go to Mass, but that they also are dependent upon it for their salvation. This is because of a miraculous event that allegedly occurs at every Mass. During a part of the Mass called the consecration, the Church teaches that the bread and wine turn into the actual body and blood of Christ. The Lord Jesus comes to exist, says the Church, in His full deity and humanity, though under the appearances of bread and wine.

In acknowledgment of this supposed miraculous change, the Catholic Church instructs its people to kneel before the consecrated bread and wine, offering up praise, worship, and thanksgiving. For this reason, Catholics also refer to the consecrated bread and wine as the *Eucharist*, from the Greek word for "thanksgiving."

Following the consecration of the bread and wine is the Communion Rite. This is when Catholics leave their pews, go to the front of the church, and receive the Eucharist. In doing so, the Church teaches that they are receiving Christ's body and blood into themselves. This unites them more closely with God. The Eucharist, says the Church, is spiritual food for the soul. It nourishes, strengthens, and revives those participating in the Mass, especially those who receive Communion.

These benefits, says the Church, are produced because the Eucharist is a source of grace, one of the seven sacraments of the Roman Catholic Church. It is the *Blessed Sacrament*, the primary and most sacred channel of grace to Catholics. Through it Catholics receive the additional grace they need to get to heaven: sanctifying grace to make them holier and more acceptable to God, and actual grace to help them do good and avoid evil.

Roman Catholicism teaches that the Mass also helps Catholics get to heaven in that it is a sacrifice for sin. According to the Church, the Mass is a real sacrifice, the continuation of the sacrifice of the cross. At the consecration of the Mass, Christ comes to exist upon the altar as a victim. There He experiences an "unbloody immolation" in which the priest offers Him up as a living sacrifice. This occurs during the Mass as the priest prays:

> Father, calling to mind the death your Son endured for our salvation, his glorious resurrection and ascension into heaven, and ready to greet him when he comes again, we offer you in thanksgiving this holy and living sacrifice. Look with favor on your Church's offering, and see the Victim whose death has reconciled us to yourself.[27]

Roman Catholicism teaches that this offering of the Eucharist *presents again* the sacrifice of the cross to God the Father. It soothes the wrath of God, making reparation for the sins of the living and the dead, and applies the saving power of the cross to Catholics.

These beliefs about the Mass bind Catholics to the Church. From childhood they are taught that only through the Mass can they experience the material presence of Christ, worship Him under the appearances of bread and wine, and receive Him into themselves in Holy Communion. Only through the sacrament of the Eucharist can they receive the grace necessary for salvation. And only through the Sacrifice of the Mass can they participate in Christ's offering, making satisfaction for their sins and those of their loved ones in purgatory, thereby speeding their release.

For these reasons, Catholics stand in awe of the Mass, revering it above all other religious practices. A ritual so shrouded in mystery that no one can adequately explain it, Rome's theologians call it a "mystical reality." Adding to its otherworldly aura are the liturgy, vestments, altar, candles, and music. The result is that most Catholics consider the Mass beyond their scrutiny. Anyone so bold as to question its validity would surely be guilty of blasphemy.

These doctrines concerning the Mass are an important part of the reason why Father Phil was so confident that Wilma Sullivan would never leave the Church. In his words, she was "too steeped in the Tradition of the

Church" to ever leave. Father Phil, however, was unaware that Lenore was not the only one raising questions in Wilma's mind about the Mass. God was also speaking to her. The Lord Jesus promised His disciples, "You shall know the truth, and the truth shall make you free" (John 8:32). Wilma was about to be set free.

Is the Eucharist Really Christ?

As with every Catholic who starts examining the Mass in the light of Scripture, there are two great questions that Wilma had to face. The first is the one that she confronted while still a Sister of Mercy. When the priest held the consecrated wafer in front of her and said, "The Body of Christ," Wilma found herself wondering, *Is it really?* The Mass, and Roman Catholicism with it, stands or falls on that question.

Is the Eucharist the real body of Christ? The Roman Catholic Church answers yes.

> In the most blessed sacrament of the Eucharist "the body and blood, together with the soul and divinity, of our Lord Jesus Christ and, therefore, *the whole Christ is truly, really, and substantially* contained—*Catechism of the Catholic Church.*[28]

The Church's starting point in arguing this belief from Scripture is the Gospel of John, chapter 6. There Jesus taught:

> I am the living bread that came down out of heaven; if anyone eats of this bread, he shall live forever; and the bread also which I shall give for the life of the world is My flesh. . . . Truly, truly, I say to you, unless you eat the flesh of the Son of Man and drink His blood, you have no life in yourselves. He who eats My flesh and drinks My blood has eternal life, and I will raise him up on the last day. For My flesh is true food, and My blood is true drink (John 6:51-55).

The Roman Catholic Church teaches that here Jesus is "urging us to receive him in the sacrament of the

Eucharist."[29] He is promising that He will give His own flesh for His disciples to eat as a life-giving sacrament of the Church.

The context of John 6, however, does not support the Catholic interpretation. The passage is not about sacraments, but about Jesus and the necessity of having faith in Him in order to be saved. In it Jesus teaches:

> This is the work of God, that you believe in Him whom He has sent. . . . For this is the will of My Father, that everyone who beholds the Son and believes in Him, may have eternal life; and I Myself will raise him up on the last day. . . . Truly, truly, I say to you, he who believes has eternal life (John 6:29,40,47).

Jesus is teaching that to enjoy the next life in heaven, a person must be fully dependent upon Him as Savior. In order to illustrate this important truth, the Lord makes an analogy between the necessity of eating bread for physical life and believing in Him for spiritual life:

> I am the bread of life; he who comes to Me shall not hunger, and he who believes in Me shall never thirst. . . . I am the living bread that came down out of heaven; if anyone eats of this bread, he shall live forever; and the bread also which I shall give for the life of the world is My flesh (John 6:35,51).

When Christ speaks here of giving His flesh for the life of the world, He is referring to the shedding of His blood on the cross for our sins. Nothing in the context indicates that He is speaking of the sacrament of the Eucharist, as Rome would have us believe.

The passage explains itself, as any objective person reading it soon realizes. Being objective about John 6, however, is difficult for Catholics. Having been taught all their lives that the chapter is speaking about the Eucharist, it is hard for Catholics to see it any other way.

I know this from personal experience. When as a Catholic I began to study John 6, I realized that Jesus was teaching about the necessity of faith in Him, not the

Mass. Only after I had been out of the Catholic Church ten years, however, was I able to see that Jesus isn't even talking about actual bread in John 6. He doesn't even mention wine. The passage isn't about the Last Supper (the meal shared by Christ and His disciples on the night of His betrayal) or the Lord's Supper (the memorial feast observed by Christians since the first century). The context is completely different. But it took ten years of separation from the Roman Catholic Church before I first saw this clearly. Since then I have tried to help other Catholics understand John 6. I have found that those still in the Church find it almost impossible to see the chapter in any way other than that taught by the Church.

Stephen, a well-informed and articulate Catholic, is one such person. We exchanged numerous lengthy letters about the Mass and John 6. I tried to help Stephen to see that Jesus was making a comparison in that chapter. Just as the Jews were dependent on the manna for physical life, we are dependent upon Jesus for spiritual life. He is the "bread of life" (John 6:35) who "comes down out of heaven, and gives life to the world" (John 6:33). I explained to Stephen how the parallel structure of John 6:40 and John 6:54 demonstrate that when Jesus refers to the eating of His flesh He is illustrating the need for complete trust in Him for salvation. Jesus is not talking about real bread or anyone actually eating His flesh.

Stephen would not accept any of this. "The eating-equals-believing theory," he wrote, "can provide no reasonable explanation for why Christ would use such a bizarre figure for what He had already stated so plainly, something unprecedented in and contrary to His whole usage of figurative language."

I was never able to convince Stephen otherwise. For most Catholics it is only after they are saved and out of the Church that they discover the true meaning of John 6.

Catholics find the Gospel accounts of the Last Supper almost as difficult. The Scriptures state that Jesus, taking bread and blessing it, broke it, and gave it to His disciples, saying, "This is My body" (Matthew 26:26). Likewise, He took a cup of wine, saying, "This is My blood" (Matthew 26:28). The Roman Catholic Church says that with those words the Lord miraculously transformed the bread and wine into His actual body and blood. He then offered them to God as a real sacrifice. This not only symbolized what would happen the next day on Calvary, but also made the sacrifice of the cross "really present."[30] Christ then gave His flesh and blood to His disciples to eat and drink. This, says the Church, was the fulfillment of Jesus' promise in John 6. And so at every Mass the liturgy of the Church instructs the priest to take the bread, hold it above the altar, and pray: "Blessed are you, Lord, God of all creation. Through your goodness we have this bread to offer which earth has given and human hands have made. It will become for us the bread of life."[31]

Moments later the priest offers a similar prayer to God: "Bless and approve our offering; make it acceptable to you, an offering in spirit and in truth. Let it become for us the body and blood of Jesus Christ, your only Son, our Lord."[32]

At the Last Supper, however, the Lord Jesus never said that the bread and wine would *become* His body and blood. What He said was "This is My body" (Matthew 26:26) and "This is My blood" (Matthew 26:28). He meant for His words to be taken in their figurative sense. The bread and wine symbolized His body and blood. That's why He used the word *is,* rather than the word *becomes*.

Even the most zealous proponents of the Mass must concede that the bread and wine look suspiciously alike before and after the consecration. Nothing happens.

The Catholic Church says that the change cannot be seen because the bread and wine change internally, not externally. They do not undergo a transformation, but rather a *transubstantiation*. This is what the Church calls its theory for why the miracle of the Mass cannot be seen. It is an explanation that is not based upon Scripture but on an ancient metaphysical concept of nature put forth by Aristotle. He theorized that all matter consisted of two

Symbols of Christ's Body and Blood

Jesus expected His disciples to take His words at the Last Supper in their figurative sense. The bread and wine did not change, but were symbols of His body and blood. The following arguments support this view.

- There is no indication in the Gospel accounts of the Last Supper that the Lord's disciples thought that the bread and wine changed or that they worshiped them as divine.

- No reasonable person present at the Last Supper would have taken Jesus' words to mean that He was now both at the table and on the table (and later under the table as crumbs were scattered).

- The Lord frequently used figurative language in His teaching, even using the same verb translated "is" in His words "This is My body" (see John 6:48; 8:12; 10:9,11; 11:25; 14:6; 15:1).

- Immediately after the Lord said of the wine, "This is My blood" (Matthew 26:28), He said, "I will not drink of this fruit of the vine from now on until that day when I drink it new with you in My Father's kingdom" (Matthew 26:29). If the wine had changed into blood by His first statement, as the Roman Catholic Church claims, Jesus would not have referred to it in the second statement as "this fruit of the vine."

- At the conclusion of the Last Supper, Jesus told His disciples, "These things I have spoken to you in figurative language" (John 16:25).

- There is nothing in the Book of Acts indicating that the first Christians believed the bread and wine changed. Neither do the Epistles of the New Testament speak of any change.

- The Roman Catholic interpretation requires the eating of human flesh and drinking of human blood. This is strictly forbidden by Scripture (Leviticus 17:10-14; Acts 15:29).

- Scripture never ascribes more than one location at any given time to Christ's bodily presence. According to the Bible, He is now enthroned in heaven. Christians are awaiting His second coming. He is not, therefore, bodily present in thousands of Catholic churches around the world.

- There is no precedent in Scripture for a miracle in which God expects the faithful to believe that something supernatural has happened despite all outward evidence indicating that nothing has happened. God has never dealt with people in this manner.

parts: *accidents* and *substance*. Accidents, said Aristotle, are the outward appearance of matter (how it looks). Substance is its inner essence (what it is).

In explaining what occurs on the altar during the Mass, the Roman Catholic Church takes Aristotle's concept of matter one step further. It claims that the inner substances of the bread and wine cease to exist. All that remains of them is their outward appearance. Though the objects on the altar continue to look, feel, smell, and taste like bread and wine, they have nevertheless profoundly changed. By the miracle of transubstantiation, their inner natures have ceased to exist and have been replaced by the substance of Christ's body and blood. Christ, says the Church, becomes present "in the fullest sense."[33] It calls this the *real presence*.

What is *real* about it, however, is difficult to understand. The Church is defining a new mode of existence that even it admits is "altogether unique."[34] What occurs, says the Church, "cannot be apprehended by the senses,"[35] for it "defies the powers of conception."[36] Ironically, in explaining why the change cannot be observed, it employs Aristotle, honored by historians as the father of observed science.

Understandably, modern Catholics are finding the theory of transubstantiation increasingly hard to accept. A 1992 Gallup poll in America reported that "less than a third of Roman Catholics believe that when they receive communion at Mass they receive the body and blood of Jesus Christ in precisely the way the Church teaches."[37] A graduate of a Jesuit seminary told me that none of his professors believed in transubstantiation.

Although many Catholics doubt the Church's explanation as to how the bread and wine change, most believe, nevertheless, that they do change. After three decades of decline, the worship of the Eucharist as divine is actually on the increase. This occurs during the Mass and immediately afterward. Catholics also gather for special times of adoration called the *Exposition of the Blessed Sacrament*. Typically, a priest inserts a large consecrated wafer into a glass receptacle. He then mounts it in a *monstrance*—a gold stand usually resembling a sunburst—and places it on an altar. Catholics then assemble to worship the host by the hour. In the *Perpetual Adoration of the Blessed Sacrament,* Catholics take turns day and night in the uninterrupted worship of the host. The Church has authorized the formation of several religious orders in which members dedicate their lives to this purpose. There are accounts of unbroken worship of the host spanning hundreds of years. The continuous adoration of the Blessed Sacrament by Catholics at the Cathedral of Lugo, Spain, is said to have exceeded 1000 years. Some Catholics, such as Mother Teresa of Calcutta, spend several hours each week bowed in adoration before a consecrated bread wafer. She reports: "I make a holy hour each day in the presence of Jesus in the Blessed Sacrament. All my sisters make holy hours as well."[38]

The sincerity of Catholics in following their Church's instruction to worship the Eucharist must be acknowledged. But the practice is nevertheless idolatrous. The Ten Commandments forbid the worship of any object, even those supposedly representative of God (Exodus 20:4-5). God has told us that He will never inhabit an object so as to be worshiped: "I am the Lord, that is My name; I will not give My glory to another, nor My praise to graven images" (Isaiah 42:8). Jesus taught, "God is spirit, and those who worship Him must worship in spirit and truth" (John 4:24).

Is the Mass the Real Sacrifice of Christ?

The second great question that Wilma Sullivan had to face was, Is the Mass the real sacrifice of Christ? This question, unlike the Catholic doctrine of the real presence of Christ in the Eucharist, is something that most Catholics neither ask about nor think about. The reason is that most Catholics are not aware that the Church teaches that the Mass is an actual sacrifice. They know that the rite is called the Sacrifice of the Mass, that it is performed by a priest, that the congregation assembles before an altar, and that the consecrated bread wafers are called hosts. Nevertheless, most Catholics do not seem to realize that the Church teaches that the Mass is a real and true sacrifice, that a prime function of the Catholic priesthood is to offer sacrifice, that an altar is a place of sacrifice, and that the word *host* is from the Latin word *hostia*, meaning "sacrificial victim."

When I told Anthony, a Catholic catechism teacher, that he was going to a sacrifice for sins each week, he denied it. Anthony's sister, Teresa, had been born again several years earlier and had left the Catholic Church. She had been sharing the gospel with Anthony, and he too now was claiming to be trusting Christ alone for his salvation. He remained, however, loyal to the Catholic Church and its practices.

"Anthony, you can't say you are trusting in Christ's finished work on the cross and keep going to a weekly sacrifice for your sins," I told him.

"But it's not a sacrifice," Anthony insisted.

"Look at the Eucharistic prayer," I said, handing him an open copy of the *Vatican II Sunday Missal*—the book containing the words recited by the priest during the Mass. "What does the priest pray after consecrating the bread and wine?"

"We offer to you, God of glory and majesty," Anthony read, "this holy and perfect sacrifice, the bread of life and the cup of eternal salvation."[39] He then added, "I don't remember the priest ever saying that."

"Read on," I asked.

"Look with favor on these offerings and accept them as once you accepted the gifts of your servant Abel, the sacrifice of Abraham, our Father in faith, and the bread and wine offered by your priest Melchizedek. Almighty God, we pray that your angel may take this sacrifice to your altar in heaven. Then, as we receive from this altar the sacred body and blood of your Son, let us be filled with every grace and blessing." Anthony studied the prayer for a few moments in silence, and then added, "Well, I never heard this at Mass."

"I'm not making this up, Anthony," I told him. "Next Sunday sit near the front of the church and listen carefully to the words of the priest. You'll see for yourself. According to your Church, in some mystical way the cross transcends time and is made present by the liturgy of the Eucharist. I know this doesn't make a lot of sense, but Catholicism teaches that the Mass is one and the same as the sacrifice of Calvary."

The next time I saw Anthony he admitted that he had been wrong. Despite almost 40 years in the Catholic Church and experience as a catechism teacher, he didn't know that the Mass was supposedly the actual sacrifice of Christ. Neither did he realize that he was not only attending Christ's sacrifice, but he was also participating in it.

> It is indeed the priest alone, who, acting in the person of Christ, consecrates the bread and wine, but the role of the faithful in the Eucharist is to recall the passion, resurrection and glorification of the Lord, to give thanks to God, *and to offer the immaculate victim not only through the hands of the priest, but also together with him*; and finally, by receiving the Body of the Lord, to perfect that communion with God and among themselves which should be the product of participation in the sacrifice of the Mass— *Second Vatican Council* (emphasis added).[40]

One must ask, What kind of worship is this? The cross was a horrific event. It was the enemies of the Lord Jesus, not His disciples, who crucified Him. Why would anyone calling himself a Christian want to participate in the continuation of the cross?

Furthermore, as the Lord died on the cross, He cried out, "It is finished!" (John 19:30). Why then does the Church want to continue His sacrifice? He died "once for all" (Hebrews 7:27; 9:12,26,28; 10:10). How then can the Church say that each offering of the Sacrifice of the Mass appeases the wrath of God? The Lord "entered the holy place once for all, having obtained eternal redemption" (Hebrews 9:12). Why then does the Church seek to continually re-present Christ as a victim to the Father? The Lord is not a perpetual victim. He is the risen, glorified, crowned King of glory.

Rome's theologians, you can be sure, have responses to each of these questions. But don't expect any simple or straightforward answers. While writing *The Gospel According to Rome,* I asked Michael, a scholarly colleague with advanced theological degrees, to critique the section of the manuscript that reviewed the Church's rebuttal to criticism of the Mass. Since Michael was about to complete a doctorate in biblical Hebrew at a leading university, I was confident that, if anyone could make sense of the rebuttals, it was Michael. I was expecting him to carefully analyze each response, delving into the finer points of theology. To my amazement, he simply wrote in the margin, "WHAT A BUNCH OF HOOEY!"

Michael was right. Rome's explanation of the glaring contradictions of the Mass amount to nothing more than mystical mumbo jumbo and high-sounding nonsense.

Even more distressing is the way the Church distorts the Scriptures in an attempt to provide a biblical basis for the Mass. Take, for example, the following reference to the Mass in Pope John Paul II's recent bestseller, *Crossing the Threshold of Hope:*

> The Church is the instrument of man's salvation. It both contains and continually draws upon the mystery of Christ's redemptive sacrifice. Through the shedding of His own blood, Jesus Christ constantly "enters into God's sanctuary thus obtaining eternal redemption" (cf. Hebrews 9:12)—Pope John Paul II.[41]

Here the pope actually changes the Scriptures. Though he modifies the wording of Hebrews 9:12, he puts his new version in quotation marks and retains the reference, suggesting that it compares well to the original. Three alterations, however, have so distorted the meaning of the verse that the pope's new version teaches the very opposite of what the original did. Before examining how the verse has been changed and why the pope would want to modify it, consider first the original meaning of the verse and its context.

At Mount Sinai, God showed Moses a tabernacle in heaven and instructed him to build a similar tabernacle on earth, carefully following the pattern shown him on the mountain (Exodus 25:9,40; Acts 7:44; Hebrews 8:5). It was to be a rectangular tent with a single entryway and no windows. Inside, a curtain was to divide the structure into a large outer room and a smaller inner room.

The earthly tabernacle was to serve as the focal point of Israel's worship (Exodus 25:8; 29:42). Each day Jewish priests were to enter its outer room and perform various duties (Exodus 30:7-8; Leviticus 4:18; 24:1-9). Once a year on the Day of Atonement, the Jewish high priest was to enter the inner room, presenting the blood of sin offerings to make atonement for himself and for the nation (Leviticus 16:1-34). In front of the tabernacle, God told Moses to construct a bronze altar upon which the priests were to continually offer animal sacrifices (Numbers 28–29).

Hebrews 9 reviews many of these details. There the emphasis is placed on the *frequency* with which the Jewish priests were to enter the tabernacle to perform their duties:

> Now when these things have been thus prepared, the priests are *continually entering* the outer tabernacle, performing the divine worship, but into the second only the high priest enters, *once a year*, not without taking blood, which he offers for himself and for the sins of the people committed in ignorance (Hebrews 9:6-7, emphasis added).

The verses that follow contrast the continual and yearly ministry of the Jewish priests in the earthly tabernacle with the once-for-all ministry of the Lord Jesus in the heavenly tabernacle:

But when Christ appeared as a high priest of the good things to come, He entered through the greater and more perfect tabernacle, not made with hands, that is to say, not of this creation; and not through the blood of goats and calves, but through His own blood, He entered the holy place *once for all*, having obtained eternal redemption (Hebrews 9:11-12, emphasis added).

These verses speak of an event following the crucifixion when the Lord Jesus entered into the presence of God in the heavenly tabernacle. There He presented His shed blood on our behalf (Hebrews 9:24-25). Unlike the Jewish priests, however, who "are continually entering" (Hebrews 9:6) and the high priest who "enters once a year" (Hebrews 9:7), the Lord Jesus, our High Priest, entered the holy place of the heavenly tabernacle "once for all, having obtained eternal redemption" (Hebrews 9:12). Only one presentation of His blood was necessary, for God accepted it as the perfect and complete restitution for our sins.

Now consider how Pope John Paul II has altered the meaning of Hebrews 9:12. He writes that "Jesus Christ constantly 'enters into God's sanctuary thus obtaining eternal redemption' (cf. Hebrews 9:12)."[42] Three changes are apparent.

The original text of Hebrews 9:12 says that Christ "entered" God's sanctuary. The Greek verb is in the indicative mood and the aorist tense. This portrays Christ's entrance into the heavenly sanctuary as an event in past time, freezing the action as if taking a snapshot of it. The pope changes the verb to the present tense, writing that Christ "enters into God's sanctuary." This makes Christ's entrance an event that is now occurring, viewing the action as something that is in progress.

Further distorting the meaning of the verse, the pope introduces it with the word *constantly*, writing that "Jesus Christ constantly 'enters into God's sanctuary' (cf. Hebrews 9:12)."[43] The verse, however, says that Christ "entered the holy place once for all" (Hebrews 9:12). In Hebrews 9 it is the Jewish priests who are constantly entering into the tabernacle. This is contrasted with the Lord Jesus, who entered only once.

Finally, John Paul changes the ending of the verse to teach that, by constantly entering the heavenly sanctuary, Jesus Christ is "'thus obtaining eternal redemption' (cf. Hebrews 9:12)."[44] The Bible says that Christ entered the holy place once for all, "having obtained eternal redemption." The work of redemption is finished, not ongoing.

Now why would the pope want to change the Scriptures? Why would he want his readers to think that the Bible teaches that Christ "constantly 'enters into God's sanctuary thus obtaining eternal redemption'" instead of what it actually teaches, that Christ "entered the holy place once for all, having obtained eternal redemption"? Why? Because Rome holds that Christ must be constantly re-presented as a victim to God through the Mass for our salvation. With each offering of the Mass, some 120 million times a year, the Church says that "the work of our redemption is continually carried out."[45] The pope, not finding Hebrews 9:12 to his liking, simply changed it. This was not a slip of the pen, but a calculated alteration of God's Word to make the Mass appear biblical.

Liberating Truth

Despite the double-talk and the distortion, Catholics are reading the Bible for themselves and discovering the truth like no other time in history. With the truth they are finding freedom, even as the Lord promised: "The truth shall make you free" (John 8:32).

Liberation came for Wilma Sullivan one Sunday a few weeks after her visit with Father Phil. As she drove to church, her soul was in torment, struggling to reconcile what she had been learning from the Bible with her Catholic faith. Tears began trickling down her cheeks.

She finally cried out to God, praying, "God, You've got to straighten this out for me. I'm so confused."

Arriving at the church, Wilma took a seat high in the choir loft at the rear of the building. From there she watched as the priest performed the same familiar ritual that she had attended some 2000 times before. This time, however, something unusual happened during the consecration. The priest elevated the host, saying, "Take this, all of you, and eat it: This is my body which will be given up for you." As he did, from Wilma's vantage point high in the choir loft at the rear of the church, she found herself looking over the top of the wafer and into the eyes of a figure of Jesus hanging on a large crucifix behind the altar. As the priest said, "This is my body," a phrase from the Scriptures went through her mind: "once for all." Wilma felt as though the Lord was saying to her, "Wilma, I died once for all. I don't need to be on this cross. I don't need to be in this host." The same thing happened a moment later when the priest raised the chalice, saying, "Take this, all of you, and drink from it: This is the cup of my blood, the blood of the new and everlasting covenant. It will be shed for you and for all men so that sins may be forgiven."

"No, Wilma," she sensed the Lord saying to her. "I died once for all."

Wilma was set free at that Mass. Father Phil was wrong. With God's help she did leave the Catholic Church, never attending the Mass again as a Roman Catholic or receiving the Eucharist.

7

"Lord, I Apologize in Advance"

Though thousands of people leave the Roman Catholic Church each year, some also join it. Scott Hahn is one who joined. Raised in a Protestant family, an honor graduate of Gordon-Conwell Theological Seminary, and a Presbyterian minister, Hahn was an unlikely candidate to become a Catholic. Nevertheless, at a 1986 Easter Vigil held at Saint Bernard's Catholic Church in Milwaukee, Wisconsin, Hahn received what he describes as a "sacramental grand slam":[46] baptism, confession, confirmation, and Holy Communion. According to Catholic theology, that was the day he became a Roman Catholic. I think it was somewhat earlier.

Scott Hahn's journey into the Church of Rome began during his seminary years. Despite his Protestant upbringing, Hahn's studies led him to reject the belief that sinners could find acceptance before God simply by trusting Jesus. After further investigation, he concluded that a person comes into a right relationship with God by faith *and* works. Salvation, as Hahn came to understand it, was a covenant with God in which Christ shared His divine sonship with a new family. This compared well, Hahn thought, with Catholic teaching.

Already an admirer of the Vatican's stand against artificial birth control, Hahn decided to investigate Roman Catholicism further. He studied the real presence of Christ in the Eucharist, the ongoing Sacrifice of the Mass, and the papacy. After long months of comparing these and other Catholic doctrines to Scripture, Hahn concluded that Rome was right about every one of them. He recounts, "I had worked literally through, I would guess, a hundred different doctrines that the Catholic Church taught, that the Protestant Church rejected, and I came out Catholic on every one of them. In spite of them being Catholic, I just felt that they were faithful to Scripture."[47]

Hahn began thinking about converting to Roman Catholicism, but first he had to resolve a few more issues. The most fundamental one was the question of authority: Who or what determines how the faith received from Christ is to be understood and practiced?

All his life, Hahn had held that the Scriptures, as illuminated by the Holy Spirit, were the Christian's standard of truth and source of all teaching necessary for salvation and life. Now the Roman Catholic Church was confronting Hahn with a different answer. It said that the faith received from Christ was to be found in Scripture *plus* the Tradition of the Church. As interpreted by the Roman Catholic popes and bishops, Scripture and Tradition together were the supreme rule or standard of religious truth.

Who was right? Scott Hahn settled this question for himself when he made a decision about another important feature of Roman Catholicism: devotion to Mary. Of all the Catholic doctrines that he had investigated, he was finding those about Mary to be the most difficult to accept. Hahn comments: "Catholics have no idea how hard Marian doctrines and devotions are for Bible Christians."[48] The latter consider Mary's role in Catholicism, says Hahn, to be "by far the most incomprehensible and offensive and patently unbiblical superstition going."[49]

Hahn's point is well-taken. Christians familiar with the Bible find little resemblance between the Mary of Scripture and the Mary of Roman Catholicism. The real Mary was a faithful servant of God who humbly yielded herself as "the bondslave of the Lord" (Luke 1:38). Rome's Mary, on the other hand, possesses godlike attributes and abilities. Her power, according to Pope Leo XIII, is "all but unlimited."[50] Pope John Paul II says that "Christ will conquer through her, because He wants the Church's victories now and in the future to be linked to her."[51] According to the Church, Mary is:

> . . . immaculate in every respect; innocent, and verily most innocent; spotless, and entirely spotless; holy and removed from every stain of sin; all pure, all stainless, the very model of purity and innocence; more beautiful than beauty, more lovely than loveliness; more holy than holiness, singularly holy and most pure in soul and body; the one who surpasses all integrity and virginity; the only one who has become the dwelling place of all the grace of the most Holy Spirit. God alone excepted, Mary is more excellent than all, and by nature fair and beautiful, and more holy than the Cherubim and Seraphim. To praise her all the tongues of heaven and earth do not suffice—Pope Pius IX.[52]

Alleged supernatural appearances of Mary, known among Catholics as apparitions, have spurred devotion to her. These include Lourdes, France (1858); Fatima, Portugal (1917); and Medjugorje, Bosnia-Herzegovina (since 1981). In 1854, Pope Pius IX formally proclaimed the doctrine of Mary's *Immaculate Conception*, claiming that God preserved Mary from all stain of inherited sin from Adam from the first instant of her conception. As a result, she lived a perfectly sinless life. Then in 1950, Pope Pius XII defined the doctrine of Mary's *assumption*, saying that at the end of her earthly life she was taken bodily into heaven.

The Catholic Church also honors Mary as the *ever Virgin Mary*. Not only did she remain a virgin "until she gave birth" (Matthew 1:25) as the Scriptures say, but according to the Church she retained her virginal state both during the birth and later afterward, though married to Joseph. The Church exalts Mary as the *Mother of God, Mother of the Church,* and *co-Redeemer of Mankind,* explaining:

> Mary suffered and, as it were, nearly died with her suffering Son; for the salvation of mankind she renounced her mother's rights and, as far as it depended on her, offered her Son to placate divine justice; so we may well say that she with Christ redeemed mankind—Pope Benedict XV.[53]

Presently, says the Church, Mary sits crowned in heaven as the *Queen of Heaven and Earth.* There she serves as the "the most powerful mediatrix and advocate of the whole world with her Divine Son."[54] She is the *Mother of Grace* through whom Christ grants all graces to the world. The Church says that Catholics should entrust all their cares and petitions to Mary, surrendering the hour of their death "wholly to her care."[55]

How did Scott Hahn, despite his knowledge of what the Bible said about Mary, come to embrace the Mary of Roman Catholicism as his own? Late one night in his office, Hahn was pondering the Catholic doctrines about Mary. Throughout his life he had used the Scriptures as his guide. That night, however, unable to find agreement between Roman Catholic teaching and the Bible, Hahn decided to try a new approach to knowing truth. He writes, "So many doctrines of the Catholic Church had proven to be sound biblically that I decided to step out in faith on this one."[56]

Hahn locked the door to his office and, in preparation for what he was about to do, prayed, "Lord, the Catholic Church has gotten it right 99 times out of a hundred. The only major obstacle left is Mary. I don't see it on this point. But I am going to give them the benefit of the doubt. I'm going to cut them some slack, and I'm going to say a prayer."[57]

Hahn then spoke to Mary, informing her of his intentions, saying, "Mary, if you're up there and this is wrong, don't be offended."[58]

Once more Hahn spoke to God, fearful that he might be making a big mistake: "Most of all, God, if this upsets You, please, I'm sincere. Lord, I apologize in advance if You're offended by what I'm about to do."[59]

What Scott Hahn was about to do was to pray to someone other than God. He was going to ask Mary to resolve an important personal problem that he was dealing with at the time.

"Mary, if you are even half of what the Catholic Church says," Hahn began, "please take this specific petition—which seems impossible—to the Lord for me through this prayer."[60]

Then, with a plastic set of Rosary beads in his hand and a booklet as his guide, he began to say five decades of the Rosary with its 50 Hail Marys, praying: "Hail Mary, full of grace, the Lord is with thee. Blessed art thou among women and blessed is the fruit of thy womb, Jesus. Holy Mary, Mother of God, pray for us sinners now and at the hour of our death. Amen."

In the days that followed, Scott Hahn prayed the Rosary several more times, each time asking Mary to intercede for him. The results, he writes, were astounding: "Three months later, I realized that from the day I prayed my first Rosary, that seemingly impossible situation had been completely reversed. My petition had been granted!" Hahn has prayed the Rosary every day since, commenting, "It is a most powerful prayer—an incredible weapon. . . ."

With that first Rosary, Scott Hahn crossed the line into Roman Catholicism—not because of the prayer itself, but because of what it represented. Consider the events leading up to his decision to pray to Mary.

As Hahn locked the door to his office, his conscience was bothering him. This is evident from the fact that he asked God to forgive him for what he was about to do. He knew that the Bible didn't teach the Catholic doctrines about Mary and that there wasn't a single example in the Scriptures of anyone praying to her. Nevertheless, he decided to do it anyway. *He did it because the Roman Catholic Church said it was the right thing to do.* He writes, "So many doctrines of the Catholic Church had proven to be sound biblically that I decided to step out in faith on this one."[61]

That decision represented a radical change in Hahn's methodology for knowing spiritual truth. Despite what he himself believed the Scriptures said was true, Hahn decided to trust what the Church said was true. No longer would he look first and foremost to the Bible. Now Scripture and Tradition, as interpreted by the Roman Catholic popes and bishops, would be his guide to truth. As to future Bible study, he would use the Church's supreme rule for interpretation: The authentic meaning of any verse of Scripture is what the Magisterium, the teaching office of the Church, says it means.

Scott Hahn's formal admission into the Roman Catholic Church a short time later resulted from this decision. Since then he has become a crusader for Roman Catholicism. He has accepted a professorship at the Catholic Franciscan University of Steubenville, Ohio, has been introduced to the pope, has had his autobiography published by a Catholic publisher, and has traveled widely, conducting seminars on Catholicism. He may well become the best-known Catholic convert of this century.

Roman Authority

The authority structure to which Scott Hahn submitted is a system founded upon the claim that God has appointed the bishops of the Roman Catholic Church as the successors of Christ's 12 apostles. The Church says that its bishops have inherited from the apostles three exclusive rights: *sanctifying power, ruling power,* and *teaching power.*

Sanctifying power, says the Church, gives the bishops the ability to make the faithful holy. This is primarily accomplished through the bishops' authority to ordain priests and to oversee the sacraments through which Catholics receive grace from God. The bishops sanctify the Church "by their prayer and work, by their ministry of the word and of the sacraments."[62]

Ruling power is the right of the bishops to govern and to shepherd. They do this individually over the particular churches assigned to them and collectively over the worldwide Church.

Teaching power enables the bishops to interpret revelation and to preach it with authority. They are the "heralds of faith"[63] and the "authentic teachers"[64] of the truths passed on by the apostles.

The bishops exercise these powers in communion with the pope and under his guidance. He is the visible head of the Catholic Church. The pope is the high priest, the supreme ruler, and the primary teacher of the faith.

The pope has inherited his position, says the Church, from Saint Peter. Christ made Peter the head of the apostles when He said to him, "You are Peter, and upon this rock I will build My church" (Matthew 16:18). Peter, claims the Church, later became the bishop of Rome and ruled the universal church. The present bishop of Rome is Peter's successor. He is called the *pope*, from the Greek word for *"father,"* because he is the father of all the faithful, including the other bishops.

The bishops, under the leadership of the pope, form the Magisterium. This is the authoritative teaching body of the Church. The Magisterium's mission is to safeguard the doctrines of the Church, to teach them to the people, and to keep the people from going astray. It claims the exclusive right to interpret God's Word and judge its authentic meaning. The Second Vatican Council stated:

> The task of giving an authentic interpretation of the Word of God, whether in its written form or in the form of Tradition, has been entrusted to the living teaching office of the Church alone. Its authority in this matter is exercised in the name of Jesus Christ.[65]

In order to fulfill this responsibility, the Church teaches that Christ has endowed its bishops with the gift of *infallibility*. This means that in matters of faith and morals, the bishops acting together are incapable of teaching error. The Church also considers the pope acting alone to be infallible. When speaking with regard to faith and morals in his official capacity as head of the Church, the pope does not err and cannot err.

Submission to Rome's claim to sanctifying, ruling, and teaching power is an essential part of what it means to be a Roman Catholic. This means, as it did for Scott Hahn, accepting what the Church says in matters of religious belief and morality, even if one's own understanding of Scripture is the very opposite. Consequently, the night Scott Hahn prayed his first Rosary, he essentially became a Roman Catholic. Everything else followed from that decision.

Growing Challenges

Though submission to Rome is at the heart of what it means to be a Roman Catholic, the Church is nonetheless finding it difficult to keep its increasingly feisty flock in line. As never before, educated Catholics living in free and pluralistic societies are questioning Rome's teaching on a variety of topics: artificial contraception, divorce, reception of the Eucharist by divorced and remarried Catholics, priestly celibacy, the ordination of women, general absolution, academic freedom for teachers and theologians, and the relationship of national conferences of bishops to the Vatican. Many of those who remain Catholic stay on their own terms, accepting some aspects of the faith, redefining others, and rejecting the rest.

Two hotbeds of discontent are Europe and North America. Some two million Catholics in Germany and Austria recently signed petitions calling for the Vatican to make celibacy for priests optional, to open up the priesthood to women, to support the inclusive treatment of homosexuals, and to recognize a "primacy of conscience" in regard to the use of artificial birth control. Similar petitions are now circulating in the Netherlands, Belgium, Italy, Spain, and France. Once proudly described as the "eldest daughter of the Church," France is now being called Rome's "most rebellious child."

Many European Catholics have stopped listening to the Church altogether. The Vatican's teaching on the use of artificial birth control is a case in point. Though formally banned by Pope Paul VI in 1968, Catholics continue to use the pill and other devices. Family size is shrinking across the continent. The lowest birthrates belong to two Catholic countries: Italy (98% Catholic) and Spain (95% Catholic), both at 1.2 children per couple.

On the other side of the Atlantic in the United States and Canada, petitions are also circulating, calling for the same changes. There, not only are the people divided, but their bishops also. Some bishops have been openly, though respectfully, critical of Rome's rigid orthodoxy. Tension between these and more traditionally minded bishops has become increasingly evident. Leading bishops have become critical of one another. Some have even begun using the press to wage their battles, much like politicians.

John R. Quinn, retired archbishop of San Francisco and former president of the National Conference of Catholic Bishops, recently called for the reform of the papacy. In a major address at Oxford University, Quinn criticized the centralization of power under Pope John Paul II. Quinn cited, for example, the way the Vatican has been appointing new bishops. "It is not uncommon," he writes, "for bishops of a province to discover that no candidate they proposed has been accepted for approval. On the other hand, it may happen that candidates whom bishops do not approve at all may be appointed."[66]

At the epicenter of increasing discontent is the same question of authority that Scott Hahn faced: Who or what determines what is to be taught and believed? Sister Maureen Fiedler, spokesperson for the progressive We Are the Church Coalition, is among those loudly objecting to the Vatican's narrowing definition of what is acceptable diversity among Catholics, and the Church's refusal to dialogue with dissenters. "Who decides what is authentic and acceptable?" she asks. "Who decides what the boundaries will be?"[67] Hoping to have some say in the direction of the Church, her group is among those circulating petitions calling for reform.

Other Catholics are supporting an opposing petition being championed by Benedictine Father Paul Marx called "The Real Catholic Petition." It asks signers to "lovingly believe and defend every single teaching and doctrine of the Holy Roman Catholic Church, as defined, protected and taught by the magisterium and the Holy Father." This petition describes Sister Fiedler's We Are the Church Coalition as "an anti-Catholic organization."

An editorial in a national independent Catholic weekly newspaper highlighted the growing intensity of the squabble. Beginning "Holy Father, We Need to Talk," it stated, "The issues will not disappear, and the tragedy is that the Vatican, instead of providing the space and means for conversation, keeps insisting that everyone simply shut up and stop thinking."[68]

With battle lines drawn and swords clashing, Cardinal Joseph Bernardin of Chicago stepped into the fray in 1996, calling for a truce. Bernardin announced the formation of the "Catholic Common Ground Project." In an accompanying document titled "Called to Be Catholic: Church in a Time of Peril," he decried the polarization that was taking place. Bernardin described how "party lines have hardened. A mood of suspicion and acrimony hangs over many of those most active in the church's life; at moments it even seems to have infiltrated the ranks of bishops. . . . Candid discussion is inhibited . . . proposals are subject to ideological litmus tests." Bernardin, himself dying of cancer and with only weeks to live, called for dialogue as a path to establishing common ground between warring factions.

Cardinal Bernard Law of Boston immediately labeled the document as having a "fundamental flaw."[69] "The

Church already has 'common ground,'"[70] said Law. "It is found in sacred scripture and tradition and it is mediated to us through the authoritative and binding teaching of the magisterium. Dissent from revealed truth or authoritative teaching of the church cannot be 'dialogued' away. . . . The crisis the church is facing can only be adequately addressed by a clarion call to conversion."[71]

By "conversion," Law means that troublemakers need to repent and start acting like true Catholics. They must abandon the notion that they can form their own judgments in matters of faith and morals. They need to subjugate their opinions, even as did Scott Hahn, to the official teaching of the Church.

Submission to Rome Is Unbiblical

Despite the Church's confident assertions and Scott Hahn's well-publicized conversion, there is no biblical basis for the submission that Rome demands. Christ never instituted an authority structure such as the one Rome seeks to impose upon Catholics. The rock upon which Christ built His church was Himself, not Peter. Though Peter was a leading figure among the apostles, he was never the head of the apostles. The Lord Jesus was their leader both while He was on earth and after He ascended into heaven.

There is no biblical record of a college of bishops ruling the universal church under the leadership of a pope in Rome. Neither did the apostles ever ask anyone to submit to their teaching without question. They taught the first Christians to "examine everything carefully; hold fast to that which is good" (1 Thessalonians 5:21). John warned, "Beloved, do not believe every spirit, but test the spirits to see whether they are from God; because many false prophets have gone out into the world" (1 John 4:1). Paul also spoke against blind obedience, writing, "But even though we, or an angel from heaven, should preach to you a gospel contrary to that which we

Jesus Is the Rock

What did Jesus mean when He said to Peter, "You are Peter, and upon this rock I will build My church" (Matthew 16:18)? If one interprets this verse in isolation, it may seem that the Roman Catholic Church is right, that Christ would build His Church on Peter. But if one reads the verse in context, it is apparent that Jesus is teaching that He Himself is the solid Rock upon which the Christian faith would rest. Consider the following:

- The context of Matthew 16:18 is not about Peter but about Jesus and His identity. It begins with Jesus asking His disciples, "Who do people say that the Son of Man is?" (Matthew 16:13). They answer, "Some say John the Baptist; and others, Elijah; but still others, Jeremiah, or one of the prophets" (verse 14). Christ then asks them, "But who do you say that I am?" (verse 15). Peter answers, "Thou art the Christ, the Son of the living God" (verse 16). The passage concludes with Jesus warning His disciples "that they should tell no one that He was the Christ" (verse 20).

- Jesus made a play on words when He said, "You are Peter (*petros*, a masculine noun meaning "boulder" or "detached stone"), and upon this rock (*petra*, a feminine noun meaning "bedrock" or "a mass of rock") I will build My church" (Matthew 16:18). The change in words indicates that the rock on which Christ would build His Church is not Peter, but someone far greater.

- Every figurative use of the word *rock* in the Old Testament is a reference to deity. See, for example, Deuteronomy 32:4,15,18; 1 Samuel 2:2; 2 Samuel 22:32; Psalm 18:31; Isaiah 44:8. Jesus' Jewish apostles would have had that imagery in their minds as they interpreted His words.

- The New Testament makes several references to Jesus as a rock or as the foundation of the church. See Romans 9:33; 1 Corinthians 3:11; 10:4; Ephesians 2:20; 1 Peter 2:6-8.

- There is no biblical record of Peter serving as the head of the apostles, the head of the Church, or the bishop of Rome.

have preached to you, let him be accursed" (Galatians 1:8).

The pope, on the other hand, expects Catholics to submit to him as Christ's representative. They are to receive the Church's teaching "with docility,"[72] treating the pope's dogmatic teaching as infallible, beyond even the possibility of error.

Compare that with how Paul treated Peter, supposedly the first Roman Catholic pope. During a visit to the church in Antioch, Peter initially enjoyed warm fellowship with Gentile believers. But when legalistic Jewish Christians arrived from Jerusalem and refused to have close contact or to eat with Gentile Christians, Peter became fearful and confused. He withdrew from the Gentiles and began to "hold himself aloof" (Galatians 2:12). The other Jewish Christians in the church of Antioch followed Peter's example and also broke off contact with the Gentile believers. When Paul saw what was happening, he realized that the very heart of what it meant to be a Christian was at stake. Paul opposed Peter "to his face" (Galatians 2:11), "in the presence of all" (Galatians 2:14). He accused Peter of "hypocrisy" (Galatians 2:13), of not being "straightforward about the truth of the gospel" (Galatians 2:14).

This incident demonstrates that the early church considered no one to be immune to error or beyond reprimand. Indeed, the Scriptures warn us that there are "false apostles, deceitful workers, disguising themselves as apostles of Christ" (2 Corinthians 11:13). In the Book of Revelation, Christ commends the Ephesian believers for putting to the test "those who call themselves apostles, and they are not, and you found them to be false" (Revelation 2:2).

Submission to Rome Is Illogical

Scott Hahn's decision to submit to Roman authority was not only unbiblical, it was also illogical. Hahn describes how for months he compared Roman Catholic teaching to Scripture, concluding that "the Church has gotten it right 99 times out of a hundred."[73] In his judgment "the Catholic Church had proven to be sound biblically."[74]

Note the process by which Hahn reached his conclusion. He *used the Bible to judge the teachings of Rome*. In so doing, he considered himself competent to interpret Scripture. He treated Scripture alone as the standard of truth. A Protestant minister at the time, he used a principle that has been known since the Reformation as *Sola Scriptura*, meaning *Scripture alone* as the supreme norm for establishing truth. It had been the battle cry of the sixteenth-century Reformation and was the cornerstone of the Protestant Christianity in which Hahn had been raised.

In becoming a Catholic, however, Hahn embraced a system that rejects *Sola Scriptura*. Rome teaches that only the Church is competent to interpret the Bible, that Scripture and Tradition together are the standard of truth, and that *no one can use the Bible to judge the Church*. Hahn has now adopted this position as his own, and today is an outspoken critic of *Sola Scriptura*.

In his renunciation of *Sola Scriptura*, however, Hahn is renouncing the very method that he used—or misused—in becoming a Catholic. It would seem that if he now considers *Sola Scriptura* to be invalid, he would desist from presenting himself as the diligent young Bible student who searched the Scriptures and through them found the truth. Indeed, if he now considers the method that he used invalid, one would think that he would pronounce his decision also to be invalid, and would begin to retry the case by some other method.

But by what other method? If one cannot use the Scriptures as the standard by which to judge the claims of Rome, one must ask, How *is* a person to know whether the Roman Catholic Church is what it declares itself to be? The Church says, "The task of interpreting the Word of God authentically has been entrusted solely to the

Magisterium of the Church, that is, to the Pope and to the bishops in communion with him."[75]

If no one but Rome's bishops can determine the authentic interpretation of Scripture, how then is a person supposed to recognize the Roman Catholic Church as the one true church instituted by Christ? By what standard are the Church's assertions about its authority to be judged? Are we to submit to Rome's authority simply because the Vatican *says* it is the true Church?

Clearly not. With the Holy Spirit as our Teacher and the inspired Scriptures as our text, we can know the truth. We must follow the example of the early Bereans who "received the word with great eagerness, examining the Scriptures daily, to see whether these things were so" (Acts 17:11).

This, of course, is the last thing that Rome wants its people to do. It knows that when Catholics begin looking to the Bible for truth, comparing Roman Catholic doctrine to God's inspired Word, it isn't long before differences are uncovered.

For Mike Gendron, a devout Catholic actively involved in the Church, it started with an advertisement in a Dallas newspaper. Endowed with an analytical mind, in his university days Mike had pursued degrees in mathematics and business. But in the practice of his Catholic faith, he realized that he had no reasons for what he believed. The newspaper advertisement told of a seminar to be conducted on the "Evidences for the Christian Faith." The instructor was Christian apologist Josh McDowell. Mike attended the seminar. It convinced him that the Bible was God's inerrant, inspired, authoritative Word. He returned home determined to confirm his Catholic faith through the study of Scripture.

It wasn't long, however, before Mike began to notice differences between what the Bible said and what the Church had told him. When these grew into contradictions, Mike decided it was time to call his Uncle Charles, a Roman Catholic priest.

Father Charles responded graciously to Mike's questions, explaining the Church's position. Mike was "pacified," as he now describes it. But as he continued to study the Scriptures, other issues arose. Once again he called Father Charles, and once again the priest was able to put Mike's troubled mind to rest.

This cycle repeated itself several times over the following three years. On one visit Uncle Charles made to Mike's home, Mike excitedly told him about his discovery in 1 Thessalonians 4:13-18 of the rapture—the coming of Christ in the clouds for the church.

"What Bible are you reading?" Father Charles asked his nephew.

"It's the one you gave me for Christmas about five years ago," Mike answered. "Here, look what it says for yourself."

Father Charles took a quick glance at the passage and dismissed it, saying, "God doesn't really mean what He says there." With that he got up and walked out of the room, leaving Mike to ponder his questions alone.

Mike's questions, however, had been answered by the priest's disregard of God's Word. No longer, Mike decided, would he allow his uncle to dissuade him from believing the Scriptures. Mike left the Roman Catholic Church and now runs an evangelistic ministry in Dallas that helps seeking Catholics find Christ.

Nadine had a similar experience. For years she served the Catholic Church as a Eucharistic minister and head of the parents' committee for youth instruction, commonly referred to as the C.C.D. (Confraternity of Christian Doctrine). When God began drawing Nadine to Himself, she developed an insatiable appetite for Bible study. Slowly she began seeing discrepancies between what the Church had taught her and what she was reading in the Bible. A battle began to rage within. Was she going to believe what the Church said or what the Scriptures said?

One day she came upon a card produced by the Catholic Church titled "Articles of Faith." It listed the major doctrines of Roman Catholicism. *I don't believe that,* she found herself thinking as she scanned an item on the list. *The Bible doesn't teach that,* she decided about another. *This isn't right either, or this one.*

Nadine finally stopped on an article stating that the faithful departed "suffer in purgatory for sins both forgiven and not forgiven." *I can't believe these things,* she thought to herself. *They contradict the Scriptures. How can I remain in the Catholic Church?*

Though neither Mike nor Nadine realized it at the time, they both left Roman Catholicism the moment they began to place the plain teaching of Scripture over the teachings of the Church. No longer willing to allow Rome to interpret God's Word for them, they were no longer Roman Catholics.

8

"Be Not Afraid"

In 1993 Italian journalist Vittorio Messori began to prepare for what he considered the opportunity of a lifetime. Pope John Paul II was about to celebrate the fifteenth anniversary of his papacy. To mark the occasion, an Italian television station invited the pope to participate in a special broadcast. It was to be the first time that a journalist would interview the head of the Roman Catholic Church on live television. To the amazement of everyone involved, the pope accepted the invitation. Because of his extensive writings on Catholicism, Vittorio Messori was to have the privilege of conducting the interview.

In preparation for the event, Messori submitted a series of questions to the pope, outlining the course that the interview would take. Not long after, however, the Vatican informed Messori that the pope would have to withdraw. His many duties would not allow him to participate in the broadcast.

A few months later, Pope John Paul surprised Messori once again by returning his questions with a carefully written answer to each. The pope informed Messori,

I kept your questions on my desk. They interested me. I didn't think it would be wise to let them go to waste. So I thought about them and, after some time, during the brief moments when I was free from obligations, I responded to them in writing.[76]

The pope suggested that the questions and answers might make an interesting book, and offered *Crossing the Threshold of Hope* as a title. A book agreement was drawn up, and the text was published in 1995. Simultaneously released in all the major languages of the world, it immediately became an international bestseller.

Crossing the Threshold of Hope opens with a remarkably frank question—one that Messori, aware that he was treading on sensitive ground, carefully formed:

In front of me is a man dressed in the white of ancient custom, with a cross over his chest. This man who is called the *Pope* (from "father," in Greek) is a mystery in and of himself, a sign of contradiction. He is even considered a challenge or a "scandal" to logic or good sense by many of our contemporaries.[77]

Messori then described John Paul's position as pope, listing his many titles: "leader of the Catholic Church," "Vicar of Jesus Christ," "Holy Father," "Your Holiness," and "the man on earth who represents the Son of God, who 'takes the place' of the Second Person of the omnipotent God of the Trinity."[78]

Messori continued:

Nevertheless, according to many others, this is an absurd and unbelievable claim. . . . You are either the mysterious living proof of the Creator of the universe or the central protagonist of a millennial illusion.[79]

Having set the context, Messori then asked his first question. It was one that in earlier ages would have been considered outlandishly impertinent.

May I ask: Have you ever once hesitated in your belief
in your relationship with Jesus Christ and therefore
with God?[80]

Pope John Paul's answer was equally remarkable. He
began:

Your question is infused with both a lively faith and a
certain anxiety. I state right from the outset: "Be not
afraid!"[81]

John Paul had first proclaimed the words, "Be not
afraid!" on October 22, 1978, in Saint Peter's Square as he
began his reign as pope. He considers these three words,
borrowed from the Gospels, an important theme of his
papacy. After explaining this in his response, John Paul
returned to Messori's question, applying the words to his
many titles:

Have no fear when people call me the "Vicar of
Christ," when they say to me "Holy Father," or "Your
Holiness," or use titles similar to these, which seem
even inimical to the Gospel. Christ himself declared:
"Call no one on earth your father; you have but one
Father in heaven. Do not be called 'Master'; you have
but one master, the Messiah" (Matthew 23:9-10). These
expressions, nevertheless, have evolved out of a long
tradition, becoming part of common usage. One must
not be afraid of these words either.[82]

Here John Paul acknowledges that his many titles
and the exalted position that they represent may appear
to be "inimical" or opposed to Scripture.[83] The pope even
quotes the passage from the Gospel of Matthew where
Jesus tells His disciples that they are not to use titles of
religious superiority or position such as "teacher,"
"father," and "leader"—all used in Roman Catholicism.
Nevertheless, John Paul dismisses any thought of impro-
priety, saying, "Be not afraid!" Like an all-wise father
comforting an anxious child with a pat on the head, the
pope assures the faithful that calling him "Holy Father"

or "Your Holiness"—a long-standing practice of the Church—is proper.

How can the pope condone a practice that Jesus forbids? How can a "long tradition" justify disobedience to Scripture? Why would Catholics be willing to accept such an explanation? The answers to each of these questions lie in the Roman Catholic understanding of revelation.

Revelation and the Church

Roman Catholicism teaches that Jesus Christ revealed the Christian faith in all its fullness to His 12 apostles. They in turn entrusted it to the bishops of the Roman Catholic Church. Known as the Magisterium, the pope and bishops are the guardians, interpreters, and authoritative teachers of revelation.

The Church refers to the body of beliefs and practices entrusted to its pope and bishops as the "sacred deposit of faith." It says that the apostles passed on this deposit to the bishops in two distinct ways. The first was through *unwritten* means, such as the apostles' preaching, conduct, prayer, and worship. The Church refers to that portion of revelation received from Christ and passed on by the apostles through unwritten means as Tradition. The second form in which the apostles passed on the revelation received from Christ was in *written* forms. The Holy Spirit moved men to record a portion of the deposit of faith as inspired Scriptures. These are the writings of the New Testament.

The Church teaches that Scripture and Tradition together form the *Word of God*. Together they preserve the entire sacred deposit of faith and serve the Church "as the supreme rule of her faith."[84]

This explanation of revelation may sound reasonable to some, especially when Rome describes Tradition as nothing more than the apostles' preaching and example. The Church even cites Scripture to support its position. For example: "So then, brethren, stand firm and hold to the traditions which you were taught, whether by word of mouth or by letter from us" (2 Thessalonians 2:15).

But look more closely at what the Roman Catholic Church means by Tradition, and you will find that it has little to do with what Paul means by "traditions" in 2 Thessalonians 2:15. There Paul is writing to his contemporaries—to Christians living in Thessalonica whom he had personally taught. He tells them to hold fast to the "traditions" they have received *from him*. The Greek word translated "traditions" simply means "something handed down." Paul uses the word to stress that the truths that he had taught them did not originate with him. He simply passed on that which he had received from the Lord. The same is true of two other verses often cited by the Catholic Church to support its view of Tradition: 1 Corinthians 11:2 and 2 Thessalonians 3:6. These verses also speak of truths that Paul personally passed on to the first Christians in Thessalonica and Corinth.

Is this what the Roman Catholic Church means by Tradition? Not at all. Catholic Tradition is not Paul's oral teachings recorded on some kind of first-century audio device. Neither is it a firsthand account of the apostles' preaching, their conduct, or their worship.

So what is Roman Catholic Tradition? It's difficult to say. The Church appears to be purposefully vague when describing it. Rome is clear enough in its claim that the *source* of Tradition is the unwritten teachings of the apostles. But source, as the Church well knows, isn't the issue. *Transmission*—how apostolic teaching has been passed down in unwritten form for some 20 centuries without being corrupted—is the issue. How has this supposedly happened? Where does this unwritten sacred deposit of information currently reside? And how can anyone today distinguish the authentic oral teaching of the apostles from beliefs and practices introduced in later centuries by others? These are the questions that reveal the true nature of Roman Catholic Tradition.

In addressing these questions of transmission, Rome is far less explicit, except to say that they each have their answer in the Church—the Roman Catholic Church in general, and the Magisterium in particular. It says that the Church is the vehicle by which Tradition is transmitted, the means by which it is kept from corruption, the abode in which it resides today, and the final arbitrator as to what is authentic Tradition. Indeed, the Church's understanding of revelation is so closely linked to the Church's understanding of itself that the two cannot be separated. According to the Second Vatican Council, "Sacred Tradition, sacred Scripture and the Magisterium of the Church are so connected and associated that one of them cannot stand without the others."[85]

In trying to grasp what the Church means by Tradition, don't think of it as something you can pick up in your hands and read. Even today Tradition is *unwritten;* it is not contained in books. It might be *expressed* in the writings of the early Christians, such as the so-called "Church Fathers." Other "witnesses," as the Church calls them, to Tradition include early creeds, ancient liturgies, inscriptions on monuments, and the documents of various synods and councils. These may express doctrines and practices derived from Tradition, but they are not Tradition itself. Neither is Tradition the result of scholarly research performed by historians and archaeologists trying to reconstruct the faith of the primitive church. Roman Catholic Tradition is not any of these things.

If you want to understand Tradition, you must look to the Church, for Tradition, says Rome, lives within the Church. It is a living thing, *the life experience of the Catholic people*. The *Catechism of the Catholic Church* says that revelation is "written principally in the Church's heart rather than in documents and records."[86] Catholic theologians describe Tradition as "the word living continuously in the hearts of the faithful,"[87] a "current of life and truth coming from God through Christ and through the Apostles to the last of the faithful who repeats his creed and learns his catechism."[88] And since Tradition lives within the Church, only the "living Magisterium" of the Church—the pope and bishops of Rome—can define it with infallible precision.

This concept of unwritten divine revelation living within the Roman Catholic Church is totally foreign to the Scriptures. Nowhere does the Bible teach such a thing. Jesus identified Scripture as the Word of God (John 10:35), but never Tradition. To the contrary, He condemned the Jews for elevating their Tradition to the same level of authority as God's written Word (Mark 7:1-13). This is the very thing that the Roman Catholic Church has done with its Tradition. According to Rome's bishops: "Both Scripture and Tradition must be accepted and honored with equal feelings of devotion and reverence."[89]

The Church is unmoved by criticism that its concept of Tradition cannot be found in the Scriptures. It reminds its opponents that Roman Catholicism holds that a belief doesn't need to be established by Scripture before it can be held as a doctrine of the Church. In the words of the Second Vatican Council: "The Church does not draw her certainty about all revealed truths from the holy Scriptures alone."[90] Catholicism, says the *Catechism of the Catholic Church,* is not a "religion of the book."[91] In Roman Catholicism, beliefs and practices can be established from Tradition. This means, of course, that Rome's doctrine of Tradition doesn't need to be established by the Scriptures. It can be infallibly defined by the Magisterium based on revelation passed on as (you guessed it!) Tradition.

Such self-validation, of course, is meaningless circular reasoning. Meaningless, that is, unless one is willing to first accept the Magisterium's claim to infallibility. In that case, Rome can't go wrong. The doctrine of infallibility itself, however, cannot be established from Scripture. It must, therefore, also be established on the authority of Rome's second font of revelation (right again!): Tradition. And so we're back to where we started, having completed the circle one more time.[92]

The bottom line is that Tradition is whatever the Roman Catholic Church says it is. It's a blank check that Rome can fill out virtually as it desires. Examples of Roman Catholic doctrines based primarily or wholly on Tradition include: purgatory as a place to atone for sin after death, the necessity of seven sacraments as channels of grace, the worship of the Eucharist, the supreme authority and infallibility of the bishop of Rome, the veneration of Mary, the immaculate conception of Mary, and the assumption of Mary.

In Roman Catholicism, if the Church's pope and bishops say that a certain belief or practice is part of the sacred deposit of faith, no one can say otherwise. Not even opposing arguments founded on Scripture will be heard, for in Roman Catholicism the teachings of the Church determine the meaning of Scripture. The Bible, says Rome, must be read within "the living Tradition of the whole Church."[93] Tradition is the key to interpreting the Bible, and the Magisterium alone holds that key. The interpretation of Scripture, says the Church, "is ultimately subject to the judgment of the Church."[94]

Catholic Bible Study

Given Rome's exclusive claim to the right to interpret Scripture and to teach it with authority, it is not unanticipated that most Catholics have little interest in Bible study. Only since the Second Vatican Council (1962–65) has the Church even encouraged lay Catholics to read God's Word, decreeing: "Access to sacred Scripture ought to be open wide to the Christian faithful."[95]

Since Vatican II, Catholics have become more familiar with the Bible, and some parishes have started Bible studies. This is the most promising development in modern Roman Catholicism. Nevertheless, it should be noted that Catholics approach Bible study in a different manner than do evangelical Christians. The goal of Catholic Bible study is not to explore the Scriptures so as to discover what they teach. Rather, the purpose is to learn how the Scriptures contain the Church's teaching. Consequently, when a biblical command such as "do not call anyone on earth your father" (Matthew 23:9) is encountered, Tradition, not context, determines its meaning.

The focus of Catholic Bible studies can also vary widely from that of their evangelical counterparts. Jean and I first started attending our parish study shortly after we trusted Christ and were married in 1975. We had learned the gospel through a home study sponsored by a small Bible church in San Francisco. We were excited about the truths of Scripture and pleased to learn that our parish was starting a Bible study. After a few months of attending it, however, we were disappointed to find that our parish "Bible study" had more to do with planning wine and cheese parties and gambling trips to Reno, Nevada, than it did with the Bible. After two years of going nowhere, we became hopeful when the parish hired a new director of adult religious education with a postgraduate degree in theology from the University of Notre Dame. He announced that we were going to study the Book of Job. The evening of the first class, however, he made a confession. "I have to admit," he said, "I don't know why the Book of Job is in the Bible. In my preparation for this course, I didn't get much out of it. But we're going to study it anyway, and see what happens."

Jean and I were stunned. How could anyone get nothing out of an inspired book! We were still attending the home Bible study through which we had come to know Christ. Dale, the teacher, was a pipe fitter with a local utility company. With a group of about 20 young adults, we were studying the Book of Ephesians. We often spent 90 minutes discussing three or four verses. The time was filled with lively discussion and spiritual nourishment from God's Word. Now our learned Catholic teacher was telling us that an entire book of the Bible was all but worthless. The comparison was striking. We decided that night that we had had enough of

Catholic Bible study and left the Church a short time later.

Parish studies can actually be detrimental to seeking Catholics. Often the parish priest's primary motivation for starting one is to counteract evangelical studies in the neighborhood. The priest, having learned that parishioners are studying the Bible with non-Catholics, decides to regather his flock by starting a Bible study of his own in the church hall.

It is not unusual for the teacher at such studies to begin by undermining the authority and credibility of the Scriptures. I have seen priests mock "Bible Christians" and "fundamentalists" as ignorant buffoons who take everything in the Scriptures so literally that they can't tell the difference between plain and figurative language. At one Catholic study I visited, the priest raised a Bible and announced, "The Catholic Church is not a Bible-based church." His words were directed at Steve and Patty, parish youth leaders who had invited me to visit the study. They had been reading the Bible on their own and bringing their questions to the priest. Apparently they had challenged the Church's authority one too many times. The priest wanted them and everyone else in attendance to know that he wasn't going to tolerate anyone judging the Church by the Bible. The priest then proceeded to explain how the Bible is a difficult book to understand, full of myths and errors. It is questionable, he said, if even the words of Jesus in the Gospels were really authentic. Wise Catholics, he advised, leave interpretation to the Church's scholarly bishops.

The purpose of such denigration of the Bible and Bible-believing Christians is to inoculate seeking Catholics against evangelization. The tactic is generally effective. Those using it, however, will one day have to give an account to the Lord, who pronounced judgment upon the Pharisees for doing the same thing, saying, "You shut off the kingdom of heaven from men; for you do not enter in yourselves, nor do you allow those who are entering to go in" (Matthew 23:13).

Revelation and the Catholic

Modern Catholics have become increasingly vocal in their displeasure with the Church's teaching on issues that affect their everyday lives, such as birth control and the ordination of women. But with respect to doctrines that they consider to be of a more theological nature—revelation, the sacraments, the Mass, and even salvation—Catholics are generally content to let the Church teach what it deems fit. Few are interested in the study of doctrine or could even explain terms such as *the sacred deposit of faith, Tradition,* and *the Magisterium.*

Recently, Rob Marshall, a coworker of mine, and I interviewed Catholics leaving Mass at Saint Joseph's Catholic Cathedral in San Jose, California. We asked them about the origin of their religious beliefs. The first question was, Where do Catholic beliefs come from?

Richard, a man of about 50, answered, "From the Scriptures. I'm sure that there are some theological interpretations that are in there too," he said, "but I would say primarily from Scripture."

Tony agreed. "Bible. They're all in the Bible."

Pat, a middle-aged woman, shook her head when we asked whether she knew what the source of Catholic teaching was. "I wouldn't know how to answer that," she answered.

Beatrice was equally in the dark. "I really don't know. I suppose from Jesus' teaching. I don't know. To tell you the truth, I've never thought about that."

Mary Ann, a woman of about 40, was better informed about origins of Catholic doctrine.

"From Jesus Christ and His apostles," Mary Ann told us. "We know them through the Bible and through the teachings of the Church."

When we asked her if she was familiar with the Magisterium, she not only gave an accurate definition, but also provided a brief account of how the Church says it was formed.

"When Jesus was on earth," Mary Ann began, "He made Peter the rock. From there we have various popes who have come down from him. And we have cardinals, bishops, and priests, down the line. And that is sort of the Magisterium of the Church. Sort of the government hierarchy that watches over, that are the shepherds of our Church. From them we learn what Jesus taught. They clarify it for us."

Other Catholics were unable to identify the Magisterium.

"The Magisterium?" said one man. "Unfamiliar with that."

"I have no idea," answered a Catholic woman.

"Don't know," said Joanne, a teacher in the Rite of Christian Initiation of Adults (R.C.I.A), the Catholic Church's program for adult converts.

"I've never heard of it," echoed Vera when we asked her what the Magisterium was.

"No idea," said Pat.

Most were just as unfamiliar with Tradition.

"I may have heard of that," answered one man in a typical response. "But I can't give you a definition."

All the Catholics with whom we spoke knew about papal infallibility, but when we asked them if they personally believed that the pope was immune to error in his official teaching, the responses were divided.

"No," said Rita. "He's a man. He has his own points of view."

"Nobody's perfect," said Tony.

"I think that he can make errors," a Catholic woman told us. "But I would really like to believe he is infallible. I know that as a human, though, he can make mistakes."

Other Catholics were confident that the pope could not teach error. Mary Ann was among them. I asked her what she would do if she read something in the Bible that seemed to be saying one thing, but the Church was telling her to do the opposite.

"I don't think that happens," Mary Ann replied.

"Hypothetically, then?" I asked. "Would you follow what you thought the Bible was saying, or what the Church told you to do?"

"I don't think that could happen," she answered, refusing even to consider the possibility.

Richard was willing to consider the possibility, but told us that he would side with the Church.

"I would stick with the Church," he said, "because of the theological knowledge that the Church has. I would accept their judgment over my own."

Not all were willing to trust the Church to that extent.

"I would have to go by my own conscience," one Catholic told us.

"I would be wondering who is telling the truth," said another. "I don't know, maybe the Bible."

Because I Like It

Most Catholics have never critically examined the doctrines of Roman Catholicism. They didn't join the Church because they found its doctrines to be true, but, as they will tell you themselves, they are Catholic because they were born Catholic. The reason that they remain in the Church is because that is where they feel most comfortable. That's what the people we interviewed outside Saint Joseph's Cathedral told us.

When we asked Vera why she was a Catholic, she answered, "I want to be. I was born a Catholic, and I want to be one."

Beatrice said the same: "Because I want to be. I grew up in a Catholic family. When I was young, I did whatever my parents did. Now that I am an old person, I enjoy being a Catholic. I never thought of changing my faith. I like being Catholic. I feel comfortable being a Catholic."

Andrew Greeley, a Catholic priest of the archdiocese of Chicago and professor of sociology at the University of Arizona, says that his research has shown that the primary reason that Catholics remain Catholic is very simple: "They like being Catholic."[96] Greeley believes that "as an institution the Catholic Church is in terrible condition,"[97] and American Catholics are angry "at the insensitivity and the incompetence of their leaders."[98] Nevertheless, those born Catholic for the most part remain Catholic because overall they like it.

What is it that people like about being Catholic? A booklet written by a Catholic priest, Father George R. Szews, and titled *Why I Am Catholic: 21 People Give Their Own Answers*[99] indicates that there are many reasons.

All but two of the 21 contributors to the booklet had been born Catholic. A common theme among their reasons for remaining in the Church was that Catholicism was part of their personal identity.

"I grew up Catholic in a household in which being Catholic simply was part of being," wrote Ron, one of the contributors. "It was a legacy, the same as my name, genetic code, and language."

Like many Catholics, Ron thinks of his Catholicism as a matter of his personal destiny.

"God wanted me to be Catholic," Ron wrote, "and that was that."[100]

Kay, a registrar at a midwestern university, saw her Catholicism in a similar way.

"My Catholic faith seems as essential a part of me as my heart," Kay explained. "Somewhere, somehow, being raised Catholic made me want to remain Catholic, even during those college days when I rebelled against most other establishments."[101]

Others said they were Catholics because in the Church they found the moral framework that they needed for life. It was a place for their children to form proper values and to learn about God. They liked the emphasis in the Church on loving one's neighbor, right living, and social justice. Others spoke of the beauty, inspiration, and peace that the Church brought to their lives.

"Celebrating communion every week is important to me," wrote Ann. "It centers me and gives me the strength I need to accept the grace of God and live up to my values in my daily life."[102]

Several also mentioned that they liked the diversity they find within the Catholic Church. They approved of Rome's willingness to accommodate everything from the traditional, to the contemplative, to hand-clapping Pentecostalism. They saw the Church as having a healthy mix of different kinds of people, all of whom were welcome. Related to this, others spoke of the sense of community that they found in the Church.

"I needed to be part of a real community,"[103] explained one woman.

"Without doubt, the reason I remain Catholic is because of the internal support I have been given during my struggles with life,"[104] wrote a Catholic teacher named Chuck.

Most of the contributors mentioned God in their explanation of why they were Catholic. Ten said that the Church was a place to learn about God, experience His presence, and find strength to live right and to cope with life's trials. Five said that they felt that God had led them to be Catholic. A few also mentioned God in passing in remarks, such as, "God works in strange ways."[105]

The primary reasons the 21 contributors gave for why they were Catholic, however, had little to do with the religious beliefs and practices that distinguish the Roman Catholic Church from other churches. No one said that he was a Catholic because he was convinced that the Roman Catholic Church was the Church instituted by Christ, or because Roman Catholicism was true, or because it taught what the Scriptures taught. Five of the 21 didn't even refer to God when explaining why they were Catholics. Only five of the contributors mentioned the Lord Jesus, and only one of these—a teacher named Richard—with any emphasis. He was the only Catholic who spoke of Christ's saving death on the cross or His resurrection. The only other reference close to this was a man who said that Christmas and Easter were meaningful to him because of Jesus.

All of this goes to show that doctrine is not important to most Catholics. They didn't join the Church because of doctrine and they don't stay in the Church because of doctrine. Indeed, many of the reasons the contributors gave for why they were Catholic would have been just as valid for explaining why they belonged to a social club or an ethnic heritage association.

It also explains why many Catholics are unaffected by criticism from non-Catholics that the doctrines of Roman Catholicism are unbiblical. Lacking both interest and knowledge, such Catholics simply shrug off doctrinal challenges to their faith.

What Patricia, a born-again Christian who had left the Catholic Church, experienced when she tried to witness to her Catholic parents illustrates this point. For months she had tried unsuccessfully to help her Catholic parents realize that there was a difference between Roman Catholicism and biblical Christianity. They refused, however, to discuss the matter or even look at the Scriptures with her.

Realizing that she wasn't getting anywhere, one day Patricia decided to try a different approach. Her hope was that if she could at least get her parents talking about their religion, she might be able to move the conversation toward the gospel. With that in mind, she struck up a conversation with her father.

"Dad, what's your opinion of Vatican II?" Patricia began.

"I didn't know that there was another Vatican," her father answered, thinking that Vatican II must be the designation of a new headquarters for the Roman Catholic Church.

It was then that Patricia realized how little doctrine had to do with her father's loyalty to the Catholic Church. He didn't even have enough interest in the teachings of his Church to be aware of the most important Catholic event of the century, the Second Vatican

Council. He wasn't a Catholic out of doctrinal conviction. His Catholicism was just "an old shoe that fit well," as Patricia came to describe it.

The same is true of most Catholics. They are Catholic because they were born Catholic. They remain Catholic because they "like it." Unconcerned about doctrine, they pass through life without ever having seriously questioned the veracity of the institution to which they have entrusted their eternal souls. And should someone challenge a practice such as addressing a mere man as "Holy Father" as being unbiblical, they all too readily accept the Church's explanation from Tradition and the assuring words of a man dressed in white: "Be not afraid!"

9

"We Got It in a Flash!"

Bernard Bush was troubled as he closed the Bible in his lap, having just finished the Book of Acts for the fifth time. *It doesn't add up*, he thought to himself. *Something's just not right.*

A retired pharmacist, now 80 years old, Bernard had started reading the Scriptures with his wife, Ann, only two years earlier. Their son Bob, a Jesuit priest, had been so enthusiastic in his reports about the things he had been discovering in the Bible that they had decided to read it for themselves. Soon they too were enthralled by God's revelation of Himself and His plan of salvation in the Scriptures. Increasingly, however, Bernard was becoming troubled and somewhat puzzled.

Why is it that the more I read the Bible, Bernard began to ponder, *the less comfortable I feel about what we're doing in the Catholic Church? Is God trying to tell me something?*

Bernard was a good Catholic, as was his wife, Ann. Together they had faithfully attended Mass each week, volunteered at the parish when needed, and had seen two of their three sons become Jesuit priests. But now

Bernard and Ann were beginning to wonder whether they had missed something. Within the pages of the Bible they were finding a kind of Christianity that they had never experienced. They began to pray for guidance.

About that time their son Bob came to stay with them for a short time. He had just returned from India, where he had been studying the Scriptures for several months. One evening when they were all sitting in the living room, Bob made an announcement.

"Mom, Dad, as you know I've been doing a lot of studying lately—and a lot of thinking. Recently I made a decision that I want you to know about. I've decided to leave the priesthood and the Catholic Church."

The room went still. It was a moment that Bob had dreaded for weeks, not wanting to hurt his elderly parents or disappoint them. But God had made it clear to Bob through the Scriptures that he could no longer remain in the priesthood or the Church that he had served as a Jesuit for some 34 years.

"Well, Bob," Bernard began, finally breaking the silence, "you know that your mother and I have also been doing a lot of Bible reading over the past two years. We're not as far along as you, but we support you in your decision." All three exchanged cautious smiles, aware that God was doing something wonderful in their family.

The following Saturday evening Bernard and Ann went to Mass as they usually did, but that night there was nothing usual about it. The parish was about to begin a novena (nine days of special prayers and devotions) to Saint Anne, the woman the Church says was the mother of Mary. Before Mass began, in preparation for the novena, the parish priest led a solemn procession, bringing a visiting statue of Saint Anne into the church. Bernard immediately began to feel uneasy.

We don't even know who Mary's mother was, he thought to himself, *so why are we having a novena to her?*

Bernard watched as parishioners mounted the statue on a pedestal at the front of the church. Then, laying bouquets of flowers at the statue's feet, they knelt down before it, offering prayers and veneration to Saint Anne. Suddenly, as if someone had turned on the lights, everything in the church took on a new meaning for Bernard.

What are we doing with that statue in the church? Bernard asked himself. *And those people up there, what they're doing is pure idolatry. It's wrong. God forbids it. In fact, what are we doing with statues in here at all? What's happened to us? And what's that altar doing in here?* he asked himself, marveling at what he was seeing. *We're not supposed to have an altar. Sacrifice went out with the dying of Christ on the cross. And who does that man up there think he is, all dressed up in vestments like the pagan priests of Rome?*

One familiar sight after another struck Bernard in a new light. Things he had never questioned now seemed plainly wrong.

"Let's get out of here, Ann," Bernard finally said, turning to his wife. "We don't belong here. I don't know why I never realized it before."

Darkness Without Light

What happened to Bernard Bush? How had he suddenly come to see the errors of Roman Catholicism? Why hadn't he seen them before?

In an age in which so many believe that everything in the universe can be explained in terms of physical science, it is all too easy, even for Christians, to forget that there is another dimension to life—an unseen world in which spiritual forces are engaged in a great conflict. The apostle Paul wrote: "For our struggle is not against flesh and blood, but against the rulers, against the powers, against the world forces of this darkness, against the spiritual forces of wickedness in the heavenly places" (Ephesians 6:12).

On one side of the battle are God and His loyal angels. With Him also are the redeemed: all who by faith in Christ have been forgiven, indwelt by the Holy Spirit, and sent forth to proclaim the saving gospel.

On the other side is Satan. He is "the god of this world" (2 Corinthians 4:4). With him are a multitude of demons—the fallen angels who joined in his rebellion against God. Also aligned with Satan are all unsaved people, though most do not realize it. These walk "according to the course of this world, according to the prince of the power of the air, of the spirit that is now working in the sons of disobedience" (Ephesians 2:2). They understand neither their condition nor God's remedy. The reason, according to the Bible, is that "the god of this world has blinded the minds of the unbelieving, that they might not see the light of the gospel of the glory of Christ, who is the image of God" (2 Corinthians 4:4).

Such was the case of Bernard Bush. For some 80 years he worshiped in darkness—the deep darkness of false religion. He knelt before idols; he repeated mantra-like prayers; he offered blood sacrifice; he venerated bones, teeth, and locks of hair; he adored inanimate objects as divine; he prayed to the dead; and he carried fetishes to ward off evil and secure favors. And although Bernard was aware of similar practices in the occult, it never occurred to him that what he was doing might be just as evil. Bernard, after all, was a Catholic, and the Roman Catholic Church had sanctioned each of his religious practices.

In those days, Bernard never thought of Catholic statues as idols. Why should he? They weren't the images of gargoyle-like demons with contorted faces and evil grins. The statues gracing the churches Bernard attended were pleasant works of art, such as that of the beautiful Saint Anne holding her daughter, Mary, in her arms. Flowers adorned their hair and golden halos formed their crowns. When parishioners bowed before statues of Jesus, Mary, or one of the saints, Bernard had always thought of it as a picture of Christian devotion.

Bernard was unaware at the time that the Ten Commandments forbid both the making of images and the bowing down to them, saying: "You shall not make for yourself an idol, or any likeness of what is in heaven above or on the earth beneath or in the water under the earth. You shall not worship them or serve them" (Exodus 20:4-5).

Bernard had learned the Ten Commandments in parochial school, but as the Catholic Church numbered them, the commandment not to make idols had somehow failed to make the list. But even if Bernard had known that the prohibition was in the Bible, he would have readily accepted the Church's explanation that it didn't apply to Catholic statues. As the most recent official summary of the Roman Catholic faith puts it:

> The Christian veneration of images is not contrary to the first commandment which proscribes idols. Indeed, "the honor rendered to an image passes to its prototype," and "whoever venerates an image venerates the person portrayed in it"—*Catechism of the Catholic Church.*[106]

Had Bernard inquired further, the Church would have told him that in Old Testament times God permitted the making of some images. Rome cites, for example, "the bronze serpent, the ark of the covenant, and the cherubim."[107]

Bernard, unfamiliar with the Scriptures in those days, would have accepted that explanation as well. He would have assumed that the three examples provided by the Church were representative of many other exceptions to the rule. He wouldn't have known that the three were the only biblical exceptions that the Church could find. Neither would he have realized that one of the three wasn't an example of a graven image at all. The ark of the covenant was a box made of wood overlaid with gold (Exodus 25:10-15). It wasn't the image of anything.

As for the other two exceptions, Bernard probably wouldn't have asked why God told Moses to make the cherubim (two angelic beings), or how they were used. He wouldn't have known that the cherubim were part of the *mercy seat* (the lid of the ark of the covenant). It was a flat surface made of pure gold (Exodus 25:17-22). Upon it, made from the same piece of gold, craftsmen working for Moses formed two angels in accordance with God's instructions: "The cherubim shall have their wings spread upward, covering the mercy seat with their wings and facing one another; the faces of the cherubim are to be turned toward the mercy seat" (Exodus 25:20).

Bernard would have assumed that the mercy seat with its two cherubim had been kept in a prominent place where the Jews could pray before the angels, much as Catholics do before statues in their churches. He wouldn't have known that God instructed Moses to place the ark and the mercy seat with its two cherubim in a windowless room at the rear of the tabernacle. Called the Holy of Holies, it was a place into which no Jew could enter, except the high priest. Once each year on the Day of Atonement, the Law required the high priest to enter the Holy of Holies with blood to make atonement (Leviticus 16:1-34; Hebrews 9:1-10). He was to bring with him a censer filled with burning incense so that the mercy seat upon which God appeared in His glory might be covered with sweet-smelling smoke. As a result, not even the high priest could gaze upon the cherubim.

Whenever the tabernacle was disassembled or reassembled during the years of Israel's wanderings in the wilderness, the cherubim were covered with the veil that separated the Holy of Holies from the rest of the tabernacle (Numbers 4:4-6). It appears that workmen from the tribe of Kohath, whose responsibility it was to transport the holy objects of the tabernacle, after removing the veil from its fastening hooks, lowered it back and over the mercy seat. They were not allowed to see the mercy seat or its cherubim uncovered "even for a moment, lest they die" (Numbers 4:20).

Neither would Bernard have known that the bronze serpent, the third exception cited by the Church, rather than justifying the making of statues, actually demonstrates their danger. When the Israelites during their wilderness wanderings persisted in their complaining, God sent fiery serpents into the camp to judge them (Numbers 21:5-6). Moses interceded for the people, and the Lord heard his prayer. He told Moses to make a serpent of bronze and to "set it on a standard; and it shall come about, that everyone who is bitten, when he looks at it, he shall live" (Numbers 21:8). Later Israel fell into idolatry before this bronze serpent, burning incense to it, much as Catholics burn votive candles before statues of the saints. During a period of reform in Judah, King Hezekiah smashed the bronze serpent to pieces in order to stop this idolatry. To show his contempt for the image, Hezekiah gave it a new name, Nehushtan, meaning "a mere piece of bronze" (2 Kings 18:4).

Previously, Bernard and his wife saw nothing wrong with statues or praying before them, repeating the same memorized prayers over and over as in the Rosary. Bernard usually kept in his pocket a set of Rosary beads in a metal box. Pope Pius XII had blessed the beads during a family visit to Rome in 1950. The *full* standard devotion of the Rosary consists of 15 decades—that is, 150 *Hail Marys* and 15 *Our Fathers*. Though Bernard found it hard to keep his mind from drifting when saying the same words over and over, he kept at it, knowing that other Catholics repeated *ejaculations* (short exclamations of prayer), such as, "Jesus, Mary, and Joseph, have mercy on me," thousands of times each day. Praying the Rosary was the least that he could do. Bernard was unaware that Jesus told His disciples, "Do not use meaningless repetition, as the Gentiles do, for they suppose that they will be heard for their many words" (Matthew 6:7).

In those days, Bernard never thought that having an altar in a Christian church might be wrong. A knowledgeable Catholic, he considered the Sacrifice of the Mass the highest form of worship. He attended Mass each week, had served as an altar boy in his youth, and had proudly attended the first Mass of each of his two sons when they were ordained to the priesthood.

Bernard knew that Jesus had proclaimed, "It is finished!" (John 19:30) as He gave up His spirit on the cross. But he never thought that trying to continue the sacrifice of the cross through the Mass might be in conflict with those dying words of Jesus. He had never read the Book of Hebrews and its proclamation that "there is no longer any offering for sin" (Hebrews 10:18). It had never occurred to him that attempting to continue to re-present Christ in sacrifice to the Father cast doubt upon the sufficiency of the Lord's offering of Himself "once for all" (Hebrews 7:27; 9:12,26,28; 10:10; Romans 6:10; 1 Peter 3:18). Neither was Bernard aware of the seriousness of the matter. Under Old Testament law, a Jew could be stoned for promoting false worship or offering unauthorized sacrifice (Exodus 22:20; Deuteronomy 13:6-11).

In those days, Bernard never questioned the Church's rite for dedicating an altar for sacrifice. This involved the placing of relics within it. These needed to be human body parts, such as a finger bone, a tongue, or some dried blood in a glass vial. The relics were to be of such size that they could be easily recognized as parts of a human body and officially authenticated by the Church as having come from the cadaver of a Catholic martyr and saint. The relics were to be placed in a small cavity within the altar referred to as a *sepulcher*.[108]

Bernard was unaware that the New Testament made no mention of Christians using the body parts of martyrs as relics. According to the Old Testament, the placement of human body parts in an altar would have defiled it, making the altar ceremonially unclean. Under Jewish law, anyone who touched a corpse was "unclean for seven days" (Numbers 19:11). Coming in contact with "a human bone or a grave" (Numbers 19:16) also defiled a person. The law specifically forbade the Jewish priests from contact with the dead (Leviticus 21:1-12). And when King Josiah wanted to defile the unauthorized altar of Israel at Bethel, he did so by burning human bones on it (2 Kings 23:16).

Had Bernard known these things, he would probably have questioned why the flat stone, called the altar stone, that rested over the altar cavity on fixed altars was considered the "altar proper." It was the location where the host and chalice were to be placed during the Sacrifice of the Mass. He might have asked himself, *Why, of all places, would the Church specify that the sacrifice of Christ was to be offered over a sepulcher?*

Bernard never thought about any of these things. Sacrificing Christ over relics seemed like a reasonable thing to him. If a church other than his own had done something similar, it might have struck him differently. For example, if a group of nondenominational Christians had dug up one of their deceased pastors, cut off his left thumb, and placed it in a wooden box beside the bread and wine each time they celebrated the Lord's Supper, Bernard would probably have labeled them a cult. But for some reason, when the Roman Catholic Church did similar things, it seemed right and holy.

Bernard felt the same way about the Catholic practice of wearing the so-called *miraculous medal*. The Church said that it was a *sacramental* (one of the many sacred signs of the faith designed to bring a spiritual dimension to everyday life). The use of sacramentals, said the Church, helped a person prepare to receive grace from the sacraments. The wearing of this particular medal was especially significant, for the Virgin Mary herself had allegedly requested it in 1830. That's when, in a vision to Saint Catherine Labouré in Paris, Mary appeared standing on a globe with a globe also in her hands. Dazzling rays of light shone forth from her fingers, representative of the blessings she was ready to bestow on all who asked for them. Then an oval frame appeared around her, and in golden letters the words: "O Mary conceived without sin, pray for us who have recourse to thee." Somehow, Catherine could also see the back of the frame. The letter *M* appeared, a cross with 12 stars above it, and the sacred hearts of Jesus and Mary. A crown of thorns surrounded Jesus' heart. A sword pierced Mary's. During a later appearance to Saint Catherine, Mary promised great blessings to anyone who wore a medal struck after a model of the revelation. Conversions to Catholicism, visions, and other miracles soon came to be associated with the wearing of the medal, and it became known as the miraculous medal. It remains today one of the most popular forms of Catholic devotion.

Equally popular among Catholics is the wearing of the scapular—two small squares of felt, often bearing images, connected by string and hung around the neck. The Church has approved about 18 different forms of this devotion, including the Black Scapular of the Seven Dolors of Mary, the Blue Scapular of the Immaculate Conception, the Red Scapular of the Most Precious Blood, and the White Scapular of the Most Blessed Trinity. Each has its own significance and associated blessings for the one who wears it. Most scapulars also have attached to them a promise from the Church of a specific indulgence. This is a special credit granted by the Church that cancels out part of the punishment that Catholics must pay for their sins either here on earth or later in purgatory.

The most celebrated scapular is the Brown Scapular of Our Lady of Mount Carmel. The story is told among Catholics how Mary appeared to Saint Simon Stock, general of the Carmelite Order, on Sunday, July 16, 1251. Holding a scapular in her hand, Mary promised Simon, "Whoever dies in this garment will not suffer everlasting fire."[109] Other forms of the legend say that Mary promised that anyone who died wearing the brown scapular would be released from purgatory on the first Saturday after his death.[110] Official Church teaching promises that Catholics meeting certain requirements who die wearing the brown scapular will receive Mary's "pious petitions, her merits, and her special protection."[111] This, says the Church, will be especially true on Saturdays—the day consecrated by the Church to the Blessed Virgin.

Bernard knew that non-Christians sometimes wore amulets, fetishes, talismans, and charms to repel evil spirits, to keep them from harm, and to endow them with magical powers. For some unknown reason, though, he never thought of Catholics wearing the miraculous medal or scapular in the same light. Not even when he saw a Catholic wearing a miraculous medal and six or seven scapulars of various colors at the same time did he suspect that the person might have fallen under the powerful spell of superstition. Bernard never inquired as to whether Christians in the Bible wore medals and scapulars. He never considered the possibility that such practices might be keeping Catholics from putting their full trust in Christ to save them, to keep them from harm, and to bless their lives.

From Darkness into Light

For some 80 years Bernard accepted the Catholic Church as the representative of God on earth. He never questioned any of the aforementioned practices. But then, why should he? In those days Bernard never read the Bible.

Sure, Bernard heard the Scriptures read during the Mass each Sunday. Nevertheless, Bernard's knowledge of the Bible never seemed to increase. Part of the problem was that the readings at Mass were never long enough for Bernard to understand the context of the passage. He didn't even read the texts himself, but passively listened as a lector read them to the congregation.

The 12-minute sermon that followed the reading wasn't much help either. The priest would often try to explain one of the Scripture readings, but Bernard rarely got anything out of it. It never occurred to him that the priest might have been as much in the dark as to what the passage meant as everyone else in the church, that it was a case of the blind leading the blind.

Only when Bernard started to read the Bible for himself did he begin to understand it. At first he found it slow going, but soon the living Word had captivated his mind and heart. The same was true of his wife, Ann. She literally wore the cover off her Bible, reading it repeatedly from one end to the other. Often she would stop and say to her husband, "Listen, Bernard, to how beautiful this is." She would then read a portion of Scripture to him.

There is ample evidence that many Catholics would receive the Scriptures gladly just as did Bernard and Ann, if only they read them for themselves or heard them preached by someone who understood their message. Jean-Pierre, a Christian preacher living near Quebec City, told me of the unusual opportunity he had some 30 years ago to preach in a Catholic church. At the time he and his wife, a former Catholic, were living in the town where she had been raised. Jean-Pierre had come to know the parish priest, and they often discussed the Scriptures. Despite their differing views, they became friends. Jean-Pierre's Catholic brother-in-law also lived in the same village. When this brother-in-law died, the priest, in a gesture of friendship and ecumenism, asked Jean-Pierre if he wished to speak at the funeral.

Jean-Pierre readily accepted. On the morning of the funeral Mass, with some 600 people in attendance, he told the congregation that death was a consequence of sin, using a verse from the Book of Romans: "Therefore, just as through one man sin entered into the world, and death through sin, and so death spread to all men, because all sinned" (Romans 5:12).

Jean-Pierre then proclaimed the good news of Jesus Christ from a verse in the next chapter: "For the wages of sin is death, but the free gift of God is eternal life in Christ Jesus our Lord" (Romans 6:23).

The Catholic congregation listened with great interest, hearing for the first time within the walls of their parish church that salvation was the free gift of God for all who believed. At the conclusion of the service, as Jean-Pierre and his wife were leaving the church, a Catholic woman whispered to them, "You should have spoken longer. It was more interesting than the Mass." A few days later the parish priest told Jean-Pierre that the collection taken at the funeral had set a new parish record!

I once had a similar opportunity to speak at a Catholic Church, though on a much smaller scale. I had come to know a Catholic priest named Joel. He caught me off guard one evening when he phoned and asked whether I would fill in for him at a parish class. He was going out of town for a conference and needed someone to lead a small Bible study for divorced Catholics. Impulsively, I said yes, recognizing it as an opportunity to share the gospel. But later I had second thoughts, and decided to phone him back and decline the offer.

"Joel, I don't think I'm going to be able to take the study. You know what I believe and basically what I would teach. I don't want to cause trouble for you with your pastor."

"Listen, Jim," Father Joel assured me, "if you stick to the assigned topic, there won't be any problem. I'm comfortable with it."

"What's the topic?" I asked, not knowing what to expect.

"God's comfort in suffering. There are two texts: Isaiah 53 and 1 Peter 2:19-25."

Recognizing the passages as two of the clearest in the Bible on the substitutionary death of Christ, I agreed to take the class.

A week later, I met with a group of about eight Catholics at Father Joel's parish. I explained from the assigned texts how God has comforted us in our suffering by sending His Son to die for us, and that through faith in His redeeming work, we can be delivered from the penalty of our sins. The members of the class asked several questions, and we discussed the Scriptures at length.

When Joel returned, he told me that the class had given an enthusiastic report of my time with them, and requested that I come again soon. When I brought the subject up with Joel a few weeks later, however, he informed me that the pastor had heard about my visit. I was not welcome back, the pastor said, because I lacked proper catechesis (instruction and formation in the Roman Catholic religion).

Few Catholics will ever hear the gospel clearly presented. They might pick up bits and pieces during the reading of the Scriptures at Mass. But, immersed in false religion, few can put it together for themselves. Even Bernard, after months of Bible reading, couldn't see through the darkness. He realized that something was wrong, but not until that Saturday-night Mass at which God opened his eyes to the truth did Bernard realize just how wrong. He later said of the event:

> We were blessed, both my wife and I, by a gift of the Holy Spirit. We had no right to have it and couldn't earn it. Unlike many, we didn't have to go through all of the stages of doubting and all the things that people normally go through. We just got it in a flash! Both my wife and I got the same gift at the same moment at the same place at the same time. We saw the errors of Catholicism. We saw the whole situation from Jesus' eyes, rather than from our eyes.

Bob Bush, Bernard's son, had a similar experience. He entered seminary right out of high school, looking for a deeper relationship with God. After some 30 years as a Jesuit, still searching, he started to prayerfully examine the Scriptures for himself.

"I prayed and prayed," Bob recounts, "for God to help me to see clearly what I should do, what was right, and what was wrong."

God answered his prayer, and it all came together for Bob. He now believes that no Catholic can understand the truth unless God first opens his eyes to see. Bob puts it this way:

> Catholics need a revelation. They are so convinced that what they're doing is right, they need God to help

them to see the truth. It's like in Matthew 16 when Peter confessed that Jesus was the Christ. Jesus told Peter, "Blessed are you, Simon Barjona, because flesh and blood did not reveal this to you, but My Father who is in heaven." Jesus is explaining for us and for people of all time that going to school, studying theology, doing good works, feeding the poor, giving away all your money—it doesn't matter what you do—none of these things can open a person's mind to see the truth. It comes from God.

For some Catholics, the process is relatively quick. After 50 years as a devout Catholic, Doctor Figueroa, a medical doctor in Guatemala, started reading the Bible. Determined to understand its message, he finished the entire book, from Genesis to Revelation, in just three weeks.

"I was shocked to learn that salvation was of God," Doctor Figueroa told me. "It's by grace and not by anything that we do."

For Doris, the process was more difficult. When her brother, Serge, and sister-in-law, Gaétane, found Christ and left the Catholic Church, they started praying for her and sharing with her the good news of salvation. At first Doris was resistant.

"How can you believe a book that's 2000 years old?" Doris challenged them.

"You believe that God is all-powerful, don't you?" Gaétane responded. "Don't you think He has the ability to keep His own Word from becoming corrupted?"

That stuck in Doris's mind, and she became more willing to listen. But when they gave her a pamphlet based on the Gospel of John, chapter 3, explaining how to be born again, Doris became frustrated, unable to understand its message.

"What's this thing talking about?" Doris asked. "It doesn't make sense. How's a person supposed to be born again?"

Unsuccessful in their attempts to help Doris understand the pamphlet's message, Gaétane and Serge prayed harder. A short time later, Doris called her sister-in-law.

"Gaétane, would you be willing to buy me a Bible?"

"Praise the Lord!" Gaétane exclaimed, excited at the answer to prayer.

"I just want a Bible," said Doris, surprised at her sister-in-law's reaction. "What's the Lord have to do with it? All I want you to do is buy me a Bible. That's all. I'll give you the money."

"OK, Doris, I'll get you a Bible, but it will be a gift from Serge and me."

"I don't want a gift," Doris objected. "I'll pay for it myself. I don't want to be obliged."

A short time later, Gaétane gave Doris the Bible that she had requested. And though Gaétane refused to take any money for it, Doris received it anyway.

The next day Doris waited until her husband had gone to work and then went out to the front porch of their home to read her new Bible. Curious to see what it was about, she turned to John 3—the chapter about which the pamphlet had spoken.

Hey, this isn't so hard! Doris thought to herself, amazed that she actually understood what she was reading. Doris thought that only priests had enough training to understand the Bible. She didn't realize that God was helping her, opening her mind to His Word.

As the message of God's gift of love for her came into view, tears began to well up in her eyes. Doris went inside, got down on her knees, and asked God to save her, confessing that she was an unworthy sinner. A short time later her husband also trusted Christ, and they left the Catholic Church.

Some Catholics need more than just their eyes opened; they need a gentle push from the Lord. Such was Anneliese, a young Austrian Catholic. She trusted Christ as her Savior through the witness of family members who had been born again and had left the Catholic Church. Anneliese, however, didn't have the faith to stop going to Mass. All her life it had been the center of her religious practice. Her study of the Scriptures had convinced her that the Mass was wrong, yet she kept going, afraid of the consequences of stopping. With a troubled conscience she asked God to help her. Saved friends also began to pray.

God answered their prayers one Sunday while Anneliese was at Mass. Having left her pew to receive Holy Communion, she slowly moved in line toward the front of the church. As she did, her conscience again began to bother her. When she finally reached the head of the line, however, the priest excused himself, having just run out of consecrated wafers. While the priest went to the altar to obtain more hosts, Anneliese waited, becoming increasingly troubled about what she was doing. Then, as the priest was returning to give her communion, he stumbled, spilling his fresh load of hosts before her. As the priest and altar boy scrambled to retrieve the scattered wafers, Anneliese looked on in disbelief. The power of the Mass was broken. She quietly slipped away, never again returning to a Catholic altar rail.

How Great Is the Darkness?

Ignorance of God's Word leaves a person vulnerable to spiritual deception, and, for the most part, Catholics have little knowledge of the Scriptures. Bernard Bush explains why:

> As a child there never was a Bible in my house. I never saw a Bible. As an adult, in my own house, I never had a Bible until I was almost 80. Now, you can't very well read something that isn't there. Things have changed somewhat, though, and I've found that today most Catholics do have a Bible. Strange as it seems, though, it's always one of those beautiful Bibles that has all the decorations. And it usually sits on the coffee table where everybody that comes into the house can see it, and the family records in it births, confirmations, and deaths. Whenever I see one in a Catholic home, I ask them, "When was the last time that you opened that Bible and read something out of it?" "Oh, we don't open it," they tell me. "We don't read it." So they've got the Bible there for looks. It's show.

It's a decoration. And they have a Bible, but I haven't found one yet that reads it.

Catholic priests are often as unfamiliar with the Scriptures as are their parishioners. Though well-educated and ready to discuss a wide variety of topics, the average priest has little experience in personal Bible study. I have met some who, not knowing the books of the Bible, had difficulty even locating Scripture references.

This lack of Bible understanding among both clergy and laity leaves Catholics wide open to spiritual deception. Without inspired Scripture to guide them, they are "carried about by every wind of doctrine" (Ephesians 4:14), unwittingly engaging in practices that have more in common with the occult than they do with biblical Christianity. These include idolatry, false sacrifice, praying to the dead, repetitive prayers, veneration of dead things, and the wearing of fetishes such as miraculous medals and scapulars of various colors. It is difficult to gauge to what degree such practices make Catholics susceptible to evil spirits and further deception. The large number of Catholics who along with their Catholicism also practice spiritism, shamanism, voodoo, witchcraft, Santeria, and the like, indicates that the problem is significant.

To what extent can the errors of Roman Catholicism and the inability of Catholics to see these errors be attributed to spiritual forces of darkness? Though only God knows the answer, it is clear from Scripture that Satan uses false religion to achieve his evil purposes. The Bible teaches that "Satan disguises himself as an angel of light" (2 Corinthians 11:14). He knows that a lie concealed within a truth is more readily received. For this reason, he often uses false religion to lead the unsuspecting away from God. Even a religious system containing much truth and promoting moral principles can be a powerful tool in his hand, as long it does not contain *the* truth and does not preach the saving gospel of Jesus Christ.

Consider how Satan used Judaism to achieve his evil purposes. Though instituted by God and founded upon divine revelation, during the 1400 years following the death of Moses the Jewish faith became corrupted with false teaching and practices. Initially, the Jews forsook the Lord, following after the false gods of the nations surrounding them. Later, under the teaching of the Pharisees, they fell into legalism, seeking to establish a righteousness of their own through law-keeping.

When Jesus came in the first century, He found the Jewish people in a pitiful state, "distressed and downcast like sheep without a shepherd" (Matthew 9:36). He went about seeking to remedy this, teaching them the good news of the kingdom of heaven, casting out demons, and "healing all who were oppressed by the devil" (Acts 10:38).

There was always a believing remnant within Israel, such as David, Daniel, and the prophets. But by the first century, Judaism as an institution was apostate. Jesus called the teachers of Israel "blind guides" (Matthew 23:16), and their converts twice as much sons of hell as themselves (Matthew 23:15). "You are of your father the devil," Jesus told them, "and you want to do the desires of your father" (John 8:44).

The ruling Jews opposed Jesus at every turn, threatening anyone who dared to follow Him. When this failed to check Jesus' growing popularity with the people, the chief priests and the Pharisees convened a council and began to plot Christ's death. A short time later, under the darkness of night, they seized Jesus. Their guide that night was Judas Iscariot, a man possessed by Satan himself (John 13:27). Jesus told the chief priests and Jewish leaders who arrested Him, "While I was with you daily in the temple, you did not lay hands on Me; but this hour and the power of darkness are yours" (Luke 22:53).

Today Satan is using Roman Catholicism to lead people astray and oppose the work of God, even as he used Judaism in Jesus' day. Just as did the Jewish rulers of first-century Jerusalem, Rome's hierarchy asserts that its teachings are founded upon divine revelation. The

Church constantly stresses its claim to historical continuity back to the time of Christ. But this assertion is meaningless in view of Rome's long-standing rejection of the truth. Even as Judaism of the first century, the Church of Rome today is an apostate institution. It is governed by a false system of authority, offers a false sacrifice, and teaches a false way of salvation. An enemy of the truth, it opposes the preaching of the gospel whenever possible.

We should not be astounded to find Satan using a so-called Christian church. The Bible says that prior to Christ's second coming, some within Christendom "will fall away from the faith, paying attention to deceitful spirits and doctrines of demons" (1 Timothy 4:1). The Scriptures tell us that the "apostasy comes first," then comes the rise of "the man of lawlessness" (2 Thessalonians 2:3), known as the Antichrist. In his quest for power, he will use false religion, bringing the world together in a common form of worship (2 Thessalonians 2:4; Revelation 13:8). This is portrayed in the Book of Revelation as "a woman sitting on a scarlet beast" (Revelation 17:3). The beast represents the Antichrist (Revelation 13:1-10). The woman who rides the beast symbolizes apostate religion. Described in great detail in Revelation 17:1-18, she bears a remarkable resemblance to the Church of Rome, and has been identified as such by numerous Bible scholars down through the centuries.[112]

Though the fulfillment of these prophecies is yet future, the "mystery of lawlessness is already at work" (2 Thessalonians 2:7). Almost one billion souls hang in the balance, unaware that the "light" that is in them is actually darkness. Without God's help and without God's Word they cannot see the error. Pray for Catholics, interceding that "perhaps God may grant them repentance leading to the knowledge of the truth, and they may come to their senses and escape from the snare of the devil, having been held captive by him to do his will" (2 Timothy 2:25-26).

10

"Christ Has Done His 99 Percent"

Climbing the steps of the bus that would take me across the width of Ireland from Galway to Dublin, I prayed that God would direct me where to sit. I wasn't disappointed. About halfway to the back of the bus there was an empty seat next to an elderly nun. I sat down and we exchanged names.

Sister Teresa sized me up pretty quickly. From my name she knew that I was of Irish descent, and from my accent that I was an American. "Did your parents raise you in the Catholic faith?" she asked in a tone attesting to the fact that she already knew the answer.

"Yes," I responded politely, feeling somewhat as if my second-grade teacher, Sister James Timothy, was speaking to me.

"And are you still practicing your faith?"

"No, I began reading the Bible several years ago and became a born-again Christian. I left the Church two years later."

Sister Teresa frowned. "I don't understand why so many people feel that they have to leave." After a short pause she added, "You should have remained a Catholic."

"It was a matter of doctrine. The Bible teaches that salvation is by grace."

"I believe that," Sister Teresa replied with conviction. "Salvation is from God. That's what the Church teaches."

"But the Bible says that 'by grace you have been saved through faith; and that not of yourselves, it is the gift of God.'"

"I agree. Salvation is by faith in Christ. Christ died on the cross for our sins. We are saved through Him."

Sister Teresa's confident replies were unexpected. She seemed to believe as I did. I decided to test her further.

"Do you think that you will go to heaven when you die?"

"Yes. I'm trusting Christ to get me there."

I asked a few more questions and found every answer "spot on," as the Irish would say. *Maybe she's a believer, a sister in Christ,* I thought to myself. It's common to hear Christians today claim that there are lots of believers in the Roman Catholic Church. I had met very few. The Catholics I had spoken to generally seemed to have little understanding of the gospel. I had never met a priest or nun who could explain the biblical way of salvation. *I guess there is always a first!*

Sister Teresa brought the topic back to the Roman Catholic Church. "Read the lives of the saints," she told me. "They'll restore your faith. And I'll pray for you."

We chatted most of the way to Dublin. I found Sister Teresa, like most nuns, to be a kindhearted woman. And regardless of what Rome taught, I couldn't find anything wrong with her own understanding of salvation. Nothing, that is, until we reached Dublin.

"Are you visiting family?" I asked as we pulled into the bus station.

"No, I'm on my way to Rome. Pope John Paul has declared this a holy year. Anyone taking a pilgrimage to Rome can earn a plenary indulgence."

The truth comes out! I thought to myself. Catholicism maintains that every sin incurs a penalty, called *temporal punishment*. The Church teaches that the sinner must pay this penalty either through suffering while alive on earth or after death in purgatory. There is one other option. Rome claims that it is the steward of a vast reservoir of merit earned by Christ, Mary, and the saints. It dispenses from this reservoir credits, called indulgences, that cancel the debt of temporal punishment. A partial indulgence takes away a portion of a person's penalty. A plenary indulgence, like the one that Sister Teresa was attempting to obtain, cancels all the temporal punishment that a person has accumulated up until that time.

Pope John Paul II, I came to learn, was offering Catholics visiting Rome that year a plenary jubilee indulgence. Pilgrims were required to receive the sacraments of penance and the Eucharist, visit the basilicas of Saint Peter, Saint John Lateran, Saint Paul, and Saint Mary Major. At each location they had to pray for the pope's intentions (his personal prayer requests). Those Catholics meeting these requirements would receive a complete remission of the temporal punishment of their sins.

I couldn't let Sister Teresa's admission of reliance on such an unbiblical practice to get her into heaven pass without comment.

"I thought you said that Christ had died for your sins, that salvation was through trusting Him!"

"Christ has done His 99 percent," Sister Teresa answered. "We have to cooperate by doing our 1 percent." With that she grabbed her bag and disembarked.

Ecumenical Catholicism

Apparently, Sister Teresa had no qualms about adapting the explanation of her faith for my evangelical ears. Her attitude was, *Our differences are minor, maybe one percent. Since we're both Christians, let's try to be agreeable. Hopefully in time you will reconsider and return to the Church.*

In years gone by, the attitude of a nun encountering a born-again ex-Catholic would have been different. She probably would have refused to talk to me, seeing me as an enemy of the Church, a threat to all that is good and true. But for more than 50 years, the Roman Catholic Church has been taking a conciliatory approach toward non-Catholic Christians. Gone are the anathemas—solemn declarations of excommunication that put critics outside the Church and the salvation that it alone offers. Gone are the dogmatic canons that condemned all teachings contrary to that of Rome. Gone is the haughty arrogance of the Church Triumphant, when the Vatican could and did intimidate kings and emperors.

Now, having lost most of its ability to terrorize dissenters with threats of spiritual damnation, torture, and execution at the hands of civil collaborators, the Roman Catholic Church has changed its tactics. Rather than calling councils to condemn its critics and their teachings, the Church now chooses to ignore them. The one-time heretics have become the *separated brethren,* as the Church now calls them, for whom the welcome mat is always out. These are wooed, rather than warned. Baptized non-Catholic Christians who decide to formally join the Roman Catholic Church no longer even have to "convert." Now, as fellow Christians, they simply "enter into full communion with the Church of Rome."

The spirit of the day is *ecumenism*—the modern movement seeking to unite Catholics, Orthodox, Protestants, and every other group naming the name of Christ. The "heart of ecumenical thinking," explains Pope John Paul II, borrowing a quote from Pope John XXIII, is that "what separates us as believers in Christ is much less than what unites us."[113] Ecumenism views the differences within Christendom as complementary rather than mutually exclusive. And so, when engaged today in dialogue with non-Catholic Christians, Rome stresses what is held in common. It prefers to blur the lines of doctrinal distinctions, rather than delineate them and thereby further the division. Every major decision Rome now makes is considered in light of how it will affect the potential of future ecclesiastical union. The Church of Rome has committees working for unification with the Orthodox churches, the Anglicans, and the Lutherans. Some Catholic leaders are talking of the possibility of Martin Luther being formally forgiven. I once heard a priest predict that the Church will one day recognize Luther as a Roman Catholic saint. Particularly in countries with large numbers of evangelical Christians, it is not unusual for the Church to adopt the very wording of its former critics.

Evangelical Knights

Take, for example, an advertisement currently running in several newspapers. It features a picture of Jesus, and a question in large type, asking:

If You Die Tonight And God Asks,

"Why Should I Let You Into Heaven?"

What Will You Answer?

Below, in smaller type, the advertisement continues:

The answer is looking into your eyes. The answer is Jesus Christ, who died for our sins and rose from the dead to make us God's children. By His grace, we become a "new creation" (2 Corinthians 5:17) and our good deeds become pleasing to God (Revelation 19:8).

What's wrong with that? you ask. Nothing, but that's the point! The advertisement's wording, emphasis, and approach are evangelical and biblical. It reads like something out of well-known evangelical James Kennedy's course, *Evangelism Explosion*. But it's not. The advertisement's sponsor is the Knights of Columbus, and they are anything but evangelical.

The Knights of Columbus are a Catholic fraternal society claiming 1.5 million members, mostly in North America. Their goals include the expansion of the Roman

Catholic Church, promotion of vocations to the Catholic priesthood, greater participation in the sacrament of confession, and the advancement of devotion to Mary. They boast of distributing 100,000 Rosaries each year. Since 1947 the Knights have been advertising in secular publications, recruiting for the Catholic Church. At the bottom of the advertisement described previously, there is the offer of a free correspondence course called *A Survey of the Catholic Faith*. This is described as the "basics of Catholic belief, cross-referenced to the *Catechism of the Catholic Church*."

Now why would a conservatively Catholic group like the Knights of Columbus want to appear evangelical? Why in explaining how to get into heaven is there no mention of the Church, baptism, the sacraments, or the Mass? All of these are necessary for salvation, according to the Church. So are good works. Yet the advertisement would lead the reader to believe that none of these things are essential. It presents good works as the fruit, not the root, of salvation. That, however, is the Protestant position—a belief condemned by the Roman Catholic Church at the Council of Trent. Are the Knights of Columbus denying Roman Catholic dogma? Have they switched their allegiance and become Protestants?

Not at all. The Knights have created a clever advertisement that sounds evangelical without compromising a single Roman Catholic belief. They are following the Church's modern strategy in dealing with non-Catholics: Stress what is held in common. The Knights have found that when promoting Catholicism in areas with a Protestant majority, more can be accomplished by taking on the profile of the highly successful evangelical movement. The advertisement described above, for example, ran in the *Southern Missouri Shopper*, deep in the Bible Belt of the United States. Generally speaking, the readership would be wary of anything Catholic. This advertisement, however, would catch them off guard, and some would be certain to respond.

But don't be fooled by the advertisement. Neither the Knights of Columbus nor the Roman Catholic Church are about to become Bible-preaching revivalists. The advertisement is evangelical only in appearance. Its wording has been constructed loosely enough to accommodate a Roman Catholic reading. A Catholic theologian might read the Knights' advertisement explaining how to get to heaven this way:

> The answer is Jesus Christ, who died for our sins and rose from the dead to make us God's children [not securing eternal life for those who believe, but opening the door to heaven, and thus providing the *potential* that some might achieve entry]. By His grace [sanctifying grace, that is, received through the sacraments of the Church], we become a "new creation" [in the sacrament of baptism] and our good deeds become pleasing to God [earning additional sanctifying grace and eternal life].

Had the Knights' advertisement stated that salvation was *by grace alone through faith alone in Christ alone,* it would have been noteworthy, a real turnabout, and a denial of Roman Catholic doctrine. That would have left no room for the Church's false gospel of salvation *by grace plus merit through faith plus works in Christ plus the Church, the sacraments, and Mary.* The way the advertisement is worded, however, leaves plenty of room for both an evangelical and a Roman Catholic reading.

This, of course, did not just happen. The Knights knew exactly what they were doing. Since they began recruiting in secular publications in 1947, some 7.5 million people have responded to their advertisements. And 800,000 of these individuals enrolled in courses on the Catholic faith. Whether these people understood what the Knights were doing is another question.

Evangelicals and Catholics Together

Rome is using this same tactic throughout the world. Wherever people are responding to the true gospel, the

Church is donning an evangelical disguise. This has proven so successful that even some well-known evangelicals have been fooled, convinced by the Vatican's ecumenicism that the leopard has changed his spots.

Consider, for example, Charles Colson, founder of Prison Fellowship and popular evangelical author and spokesman. In 1990, Colson wrote the foreword to a book titled *Evangelical Catholics*. According to the author, Roman Catholic Keith Fournier, the purpose of the book is to call Catholics and Protestants together: "We must see that we were meant to be one church united under one Head."[114] Colson writes in the foreword:

> It's high time that all of us who are Christians come together regardless of the difference of our confessions and our traditions and make common cause to bring Christian values to bear in our society. When the barbarians are scaling the walls, there is no time for petty quarreling in the camp. . . . We have much to forgive, much to relearn.[115]

Colson knows that evangelical Protestants and Roman Catholics don't hold to the same beliefs. But, at least in his mind, the differences amount to nothing more than "petty quarreling." As he sees it, the time has come to forgive, to forget, and to work together.

Colson picked up that same theme in his 1992 book, *The Body*. There he writes:

> In recent decades, Catholic and Protestant doctrine has dramatically converged. In the fall of 1991, Pope John Paul II and Lutheran bishops from Scandinavia joined in an ecumenical celebration—not ignoring differences, but emphasizing growing unity on matters of orthodoxy, including justification. In his message, the Swedish primate said: "dialogue has proven the existence of a basic unity for instance in the question of justification by faith, to which the pope agreed that both sides were 'very close' to a common understanding."[116]

If there has been a convergence of doctrine between Catholics and Protestants, as Colson contends, then all movement has been on the part of the latter. Rome has not changed, and it is not about to change. Indeed, the Catholic Church cannot change. Having dogmatically decreed itself to be infallible, incapable of doctrinal error, it cannot admit to one false teaching without risking the collapse of its entire authority structure.

The Roman Catholic Church has not been changing its doctrines but, as Catholic theologians describe it, *reformulating* its answers. The result is that while remaining unchanged, it *appears* more evangelical. One can easily be fooled, even as I was by Sister Teresa. But peek behind the mask that the Church wears when interacting with evangelicals, and you will discover Catholicism's true identity. It is in the Church's in-house teaching that the real doctrines and intents of the Church are to be found. Read the *Catechism of the Catholic Church,* the writings of Pope John Paul II, and current Catholic periodicals. There you will find that, far from moving toward biblical Christianity, Rome is becoming more traditional, more dogmatic, and increasingly intolerant of divergent views within the Church.

Evangelical Christians should have been shocked by the ecumenical thrust of *The Body.* The book instead became a Christian bestseller. Even Colson was somewhat unprepared for *The Body*'s widespread acceptance, commenting, "That reflection on biblical themes of the Church and unity in Christ captured the evangelical imagination, strengthening our intuition that the time had come to take the initiative that would eventually produce E.C.T."[117]

E.C.T. *(Evangelicals and Catholics Together)* is an ecumenical accord spearheaded by Charles Colson and Roman Catholic priest Richard John Neuhaus, a former Lutheran minister who converted to Roman Catholicism. Made public in 1994, the signers of this document apologized for past hostilities: "We together, Evangelicals and Catholics, confess our sins against the unity that Christ intends for all his disciples." They declared their unity: "Evangelicals and Catholics are brothers and sisters in Christ." The signers also promised to refrain from evangelizing one another's flocks, labeling such activity as "sheep stealing," and pledging to begin witnessing together so as to prepare the world for the second coming of Christ. Among those joining Charles Colson in signing E.C.T. were evangelicals J. I. Packer (Regent College), Bill Bright (Campus Crusade for Christ), Pat Robertson (Regent University), Os Guinness (Trinity Forum), Richard Mouw (Fuller Theological Seminary), and Mark Noll (Wheaton College).

Other leading evangelicals were outraged. Dave Hunt labeled *Evangelicals and Catholics Together* a betrayal of the Reformation. John MacArthur, describing the Roman Catholic Church as an apostate form of Christianity, called upon the evangelical signers to recant. Others also strongly objected to the document, including R. C. Sproul, James Kennedy, and John Ankerberg.

Responding to growing criticism, J. I. Packer wrote a defense of E.C.T. that was published in *Christianity Today* titled "Why I Signed It." There Packer wrote, "Do we recognize that good evangelical Protestants and good Roman Catholics—good, I mean, in terms of their own church's stated ideal of spiritual life—are Christians together? We ought to recognize this, for it is true."[118]

It is not true. What it means to be a "good Roman Catholic" is defined in the *Catechism of the Catholic Church*. There you will find a false gospel of infant baptismal justification, good works and sacraments that improve one's standing before God, a merit system whereby Catholics working in cooperation with grace can earn eternal life, and a reaffirmation of purgatory as a place where Catholics must atone for their sins. Roman Catholicism rejects justification by faith alone through the imputed righteousness of Christ.

Undaunted by criticism and rebuke, Colson wrote the following year, "We are regularly asked whether we are pleased with the response to E.C.T. Pleased is not the word for it. We are immeasurably grateful to God for what he has done and continues to do through this initiative."[119]

Colson continues: "Our work is far from done. As we said, E.C.T. is only a beginning. We do believe this effort has been blessed by God, and we are gratified beyond measure by the reception it has received from innumerable evangelical and Catholic Christians."[120]

Where is the ecumenical movement heading? J. I. Packer argues that to some degree it has already achieved its goal. Catholics and Protestants are already standing side by side in opposition to issues such as abortion, working together in evangelism, and joining for worship. Packer writes:

> Billy Graham's cooperative evangelism, in which all the churches in an area, of whatever stripe, are invited to share, is well established on today's Christian scene. And so are charismatic get-togethers, some of them one-off, some of them regular, and some of them huge, where the distinction between Protestant and Catholic vanishes in a Christ-centered unity of experience.[121]

He concludes: "So the togetherness that E.C.T. pleads for has already begun. E.C.T., then, must be viewed as fuel for a fire that is already alight."[122]

How does Rome and its exclusive claim to being the one, holy, Catholic, and apostolic church instituted by Christ fit into this growing fraternity? Packer says it's just fine: "In the days when Rome seemed to aim at political control of all Christendom and the death of Protestant churches, such partnership was not possible. But those days are past and after Vatican II can hardly return."[123]

Packer is right in stating that ecumenical unity is already becoming a reality. But as to the ambitions of Rome in joining hands with evangelicals, he is mistaken. The Catholic Church has never dropped its claim to the "control of all Christendom." In its recently released *Catechism of the Catholic Church*, the Vatican states: "For the Roman Pontiff, by reason of his office as Vicar of Christ, and as pastor of the entire Church has full, supreme, and universal power over the whole Church, a power which he can always exercise unhindered."[124] In its "Decree on Ecumenism," the Second Vatican Council unabashedly stated that its goal in working toward unity is that all would return to the Roman Catholic Church:

> The results will be that, little by little, as the obstacles to perfect ecclesiastical communion are overcome, all Christians will be gathered, in a common celebration of the Eucharist, into the unity of the one and only Church, which Christ bestowed on his Church from the beginning. This unity, we believe, subsists in the Catholic Church as something she can never lose, and we hope that it will continue to increase until the end of time—Second Vatican Council.[125]

Mimics of the Truth

Bible-believing Christians should know better than to be fooled by Rome's ecumenical facade. The Scriptures warn us that in the end times the greatest threat to the truth will not come from hostile atheistic governments but from false teachers claiming to be Christians (1 Timothy 4:1-3; 2 Timothy 3:1-9; 2 Peter 2:1-3). These will "secretly introduce destructive heresies" (2 Peter 2:1) into the true Church. It will be a time of apostasy in which "some will fall away from the faith" (1 Timothy 4:1). The Bible tells us that the tactic these false teachers will use will be an old and familiar one: "Just as Jannes and ambres opposed Moses, so these men also oppose the truth, men of depraved mind, rejected as regards the faith" (2 Timothy 3:8). Jannes and Jambres were the magicians who kept Pharaoh from listening to Moses. When Moses threw down his staff before Pharaoh and it became a serpent, "the magicians of Egypt did the same with their secret arts" (Exodus 7:11). The same thing happened when Moses turned water into blood, and when he brought frogs up on the land (Exodus 7:20-22; 8:5-7). The magicians did what Moses did. Pharaoh, seeing no difference between Moses and his court magicians, refused to listen to Moses.

Scripture says that "just as" the magicians opposed Moses, "so" the false teachers of the last days will oppose the truth. They will use the same method: mimicry. They will not be atheists, proclaiming that God is dead. They will not be enemies of religion, burning Bibles and imprisoning Christians. To the contrary, they will carry large Bibles and quote them freely. They will talk of God, salvation, grace, and truth. Outwardly they will hold to "a form of godliness" (2 Timothy 3:5), but inwardly they will deny its power.

The outcome of these false teachers is also predicted in the Bible: "They will not make further progress; for their folly will be obvious to all, as also that of those two [magicians] came to be" (2 Timothy 3:9). Jannes and Jambres were able to mimic Moses' first three signs, but they failed to duplicate the fourth. When Moses told Aaron to strike the earth with his staff, "all the dust of the earth became gnats through all the land of Egypt" (Exodus 8:17). Scripture says that the "magicians tried with their secret arts to bring forth gnats, but they could not" (Exodus 8:18). Jannes and Jambres confessed in their failure, "This is the finger of God" (Exodus 8:19).

Similarly, the Roman Catholic Church can imitate true Christianity, but only so far. Its false gospel cannot bring forth genuine spiritual life from dead sinners. In a future day, its folly will become obvious to all, even as that of the two magicians came to be.

Notes

1. Jessa Vartanian, "A New Leaf," *San Jose Mercury News*, January 19, 1997, G2. Used with permission.

2. Pope John Paul II, *Salvifici Doloris*. See also *Catechism of the Catholic Church,* nos. 618, 964, 1505, 1521, 1532.

3. Liturgy of the Mass, the Penitential Rite.

4. *Catechism of the Catholic Church,* no. 1128.

5. Don Lattin, "Priest Pleads Not Guilty to Molestations," *San Francisco Chronicle,* January 26, 1995, A15.

6. Reported by the Scripps Howard News Service and carried in the *Oakland Tribune,* November 19, 1994, A16, in an article titled "Catholic Priest Dies from Heart Attack in Gay Bathhouse."

7. *The Code of Canon Law*, canon 1247.

8. Ibid., canon 1248.

9. Thomas Day, *Why Catholics Can't Sing* (New York: Crossroad Publishing Company, 1990), p. 3.

10. Ibid., p. 82, quoting Mark Searle, "The Notre Dame Study of Catholic Parish Life," *Worship,* vol. 60, no. 4 (July 1986).

11. Ibid.

12. *New York Times,* February 1, 1990, B4.

13. *The Rites of the Catholic Church* (New York: Pueblo Publishing Co., 1990), vol. 1, pp. 1077-78.

14. Ibid., p. 1076.

15. Ibid.

16. Ibid., p. 946.

17. Council of Florence, session 11. See also *Catechism of the Catholic Church,* no. 1026.

18. *Catechism of the Catholic Church*, no. 1026.

19. *Christianity Today* (March 6, 1995).

20. Father William J. Cogan, *A Catechism for Adults* (Youngstown: Cogan Productions, 1975), p. 50.

21. Second Vatican Council, *Dogmatic Constitution on the Church,* chapter 2, no. 14.

22. "If anyone says that a person is absolved from sins and is justified by the fact that he certainly believes he is absolved and justified; or that no one is truly justified except one who believes that he is justified, and that by that faith alone are forgiveness and justification effected: let him be anathema" (Council of Trent, "Canons Concerning Justification," session 6, no. 14).

   "If anyone says that justice once received is neither preserved nor increased in the sight of God by good works, but that the works themselves are no more than the effects and signs of the justification obtained, and not also a cause of its increase: let him be anathema" (Council of Trent, "Canons Concerning Justification," session 6, no. 24).

23. Second Vatican Council, "Dogmatic Constitution on the Church," no. 51.

24. The Code of Canon Law, canon 1364. The Church defines *apostasy* as "the total repudiation of the Christian faith" (canon 751). *Heresy* is "the obstinate post-baptismal denial of some truth which must be believed with divine and catholic faith, or it is likewise an obstinate doubt concerning the same" (canon 751). *Schism* is "the refusal of submission to the Roman Pontiff or of communion with the members of the Church subject to him" (canon 751).

25. Second Vatican Council, "Sacred Liturgy," *On Holy Communion and the Worship of the Eucharistic Mystery Outside of Mass,* no. 79.

26. Second Vatican Council, "Sacred Liturgy," *Instruction on Facilitating Sacramental Eucharistic Communion in Particular Circumstances,* introduction.

27. The Memorial Prayer of the Third Eucharistic Prayer.

28. *Catechism of the Catholic Church,* no. 1374, quoting the Council of Trent.

29. Ibid., no. 1384.

30. Ibid., no. 621.

31. Liturgy of the Eucharist, Preparation of the Altar and the Gifts.

32. Liturgy of the Eucharist, Eucharistic Prayer I.

33. *Catechism of the Catholic Church,* no. 1374.

34. Second Vatican Council, "Sacred Liturgy," *On Holy Communion and the Worship of the Eucharistic Mystery Outside of Mass,* no. 6.

35. *Catechism of the Catholic Church,* no. 1381, quoting Thomas Aquinas.

36. John A. McHugh, O.P., and Charles J. Callan, O.P., translators, *The Roman Catechism: The Catechism of the Council of Trent* (Rockford, IL: Tan Books and Publishers, 1982), p. 239.

37. "Many Catholics Disagree on Transubstantiation," *Catholic Voice,* June 15, 1992.

38. Quoted by Thaddine Chopp, "Devoted Once More," *Our Sunday Visitor,* November 24, 1996, p. 20.

39. Liturgy of the Eucharist, First Eucharistic Prayer, the Memorial Prayer.

40. Second Vatican Council, "Sacred Liturgy," *Second Instruction on the Proper Implementation of the Constitution on the Sacred Liturgy,* no. 12.

41. Pope John Paul II, *Crossing the Threshold of Hope* (New York: Knopf, 1995), p. 139.

42. Ibid.

43. Ibid.

44. Ibid.

45. Second Vatican Council, "Life of Priests," no. 13. See also the Code of Canon Law, canon 904.

46. The story of Scott Hahn's conversion to Roman Catholicism is based on a book by Scott and Kimberly Hahn, *Rome Sweet Home* (San Francisco: Igna-tius Press, 1993), pp. 67-68, 91, and an audiotape by Scott Hahn, *Protestant Minister Becomes Catholic* (West Covina, CA: Saint Joseph Communications).

47. Hahn, *Protestant Minister Becomes Catholic* audiotape.

48. Hahn, *Rome Sweet Home,* p. 67.

49. Hahn, *Protestant Minister Becomes Catholic* audiotape.

50. Pope Leo XIII, *Adiutricem Populi.*

51. Pope John Paul II, *Crossing the Threshold of Hope,* p. 221.

52. Pope Pius IX, *Ineffabilis Deus.*

53. Pope Benedict XV, *Inter Sodalicia.*

54. Pope Pius X, *Ad Diem Illum Laetissimum,* no. 13.

55. *Catechism of the Catholic Church,* no. 2677.

56. Hahn, *Rome Sweet Home,* p. 67.

57. Combined quotes from Hahn, *Rome Sweet Home,* pp. 67-68, and Hahn, *Protestant Minister Becomes Catholic* audiotape.

58. Hahn, *Protestant Minister Becomes Catholic* audiotape.

59. Combined quotes from Hahn, *Rome Sweet Home,* pp. 67-68, and Hahn, *Protestant Minister Becomes Catholic* audiotape.

60. Hahn, *Rome Sweet Home,* pp. 67-68.

61. Hahn, *Rome Sweet Home,* p. 67.

62. *Catechism of the Catholic Church,* no. 893.

63. Ibid., no. 888.

64. Ibid.

65. Second Vatican Council, "Dogmatic Constitution on Divine Revelation," no. 10.

66. Archbishop John R. Quinn, lecture at Campion Hall, Oxford, June 29, 1996.

67. Pamela Schaeffer, "Initiative seeks 'Catholic Common Ground,'" *National Catholic Reporter,* August 23, 1996, p. 3.

68. "This Fractious Family Wants to Sit Down and Talk," *National Catholic Reporter,* October 13, 1995, p. 20.

69. Quoted by Schaeffer, "Initiative Seeks," p. 3.

70. Ibid.

71. Ibid.

72. *Catechism of the Catholic Church,* no. 87.

73. Hahn, *Rome Sweet Home,* p. 67.

74. Ibid.

75. *Catechism of the Catholic Church,* no. 100.

76. John Paul II, *Crossing the Threshold of Hope,* p. vi.

77. Ibid., p. 3.

78. Ibid., pp. 3-4.

79. Ibid., p. 4.

80. Ibid.

81. Ibid.

82. Ibid., p. 6.

83. Most Roman Catholic titles of religious office are prohibited by Matthew 23:6-10. These include *father, abbot* (meaning "father"); *doctor* (meaning "teacher"); *monsignor* (meaning "my lord"); and *pope* (meaning "father"). This can create some awkward situations for Christians who interact frequently with Catholics and yet wish to obey the Lord's command. Some priests will allow non-Catholics with whom they are well-acquainted to address them by their first names. Another alternative is to substitute *reverend* ("worthy of respect") for *father.* This is an acceptable alternative among Catholics. However, though *reverend* is not explicitly forbidden by the letter of Matthew 23:6-10, it may be by the spirit of the command. In my writings, I have chosen for the sake of clarity to refer to Catholic clergy by their common Catholic titles, seeking to communicate how they think of themselves and how others generally refer to them. In my personal interaction with Catholic clergy, I avoid the use of all religious titles.

84. Second Vatican Council, "Dogmatic Constitution on Divine Revelation," no. 21.

85. Ibid., no. 10, or see *Catechism of the Catholic Church*, no. 95.

86. *Catechism of the Catholic Church*, no. 113.

87. The German Bishop's Conference, *The Church's Confession of Faith* (San Francisco, CA: Ignatius Press, 1987), p. 45, quoting J. A. Möhler. See also the Second Vatican Council, "Dogmatic Constitution on Divine Revelation," no. 8; and the Council of Trent, session 4, "First Decree: Acceptance of the Sacred Books and Apostolic Traditions."

88. Jean Bainvel, *The Catholic Encyclopedia* (New York: Robert Appleton Co., 1912), "Tradition," vol. 15, p. 9.

89. Second Vatican Council, "Dogmatic Constitution on Divine Revelation," no. 9.

90. Ibid.

91. *Catechism of the Catholic Church,* no. 108, quoting the Second Vatican Council, "Dogmatic Constitution on Divine Revelation," no. 11.

92. Some have accused Christians of using similar circular reasoning in arguing for the authority and inspiration of Scripture when they say things such as: "I know the Bible is inspired because it says it's inspired." Such reasoning, critics point out, is fallacious.

The point is well-taken. Nevertheless, there are valid reasons for believing in the authority and inspiration of the Scriptures. As others have demonstrated, ultimately it is Jesus Christ who establishes the Bible as the inspired and authoritative Word of God. The argument goes as follows: Textual and historical evidence show the New Testament to be a reliable and trustworthy document. In the New Testament is found a record of events related to the life and teaching of Jesus Christ. These provide sufficient evidence to believe with confidence that Jesus Christ is the Son of God. Jesus Christ as the divine Son of God is an infallible authority. He taught that the Scriptures are the Word of God. As the Word of God, the Bible is infallible, supremely authoritative, and utterly trustworthy.

93. *Catechism of the Catholic Church,* no. 113.

94. Ibid., no. 119, quoting the Second Vatican Council, "Dogmatic Constitution on Divine Revelation," no. 12.

95. Second Vatican Council, "Dogmatic Constitution on Divine Revelation," no. 22.

96. Andrew M. Greeley, *The Catholic Myth* (New York: Charles Scribner's Sons, 1990), p. 3.

97. Ibid., p. 4.

98. Ibid., p. 6.

99. George R. Szews, ed.; *Why I Am Catholic* (Chicago: ACTA Publications, 1996).

100.   Ibid., pp. 39-40.

101.   Ibid., p. 24.

102.   Ibid., p. 26.

103.   Ibid., pp. 8-9.

104.   Ibid., p. 44.

105.   Ibid., p. 12.

106.   *Catechism of the Catholic Church*, no. 2132, quoting Saint Basil and the Council of Nicaea II.

107.   *Catechism of the Catholic Church*, no. 2130.

108.   Under the Code of Canon Law in effect from 1917 to 1983, every altar was to be constructed with a small space, called the *sepulcher*, into which were to be placed the relics of saints (Code of Canon Law of 1917, canon 1198, section 4). Current Canon Law states: "The ancient tradition of keeping the relics of martyrs and other saints under a fixed altar is to be preserved according to the norms give in the liturgical books" (Code of Canon Law of 1983, canon 1237, section 2). No longer must relics be placed *in* the altar; *under* is sufficient. A movable or portable altar is now exempt from the requirement.

109.   Joseph Hilgers, *The Catholic Encyclopedia* (New York: Robert Appleton Co., 1912), "Scapular," vol. 13, p. 511.

110.   Alphonsus De Liguori, *The Glories of Mary* (Brooklyn, NY: Redemptorist Fathers, 1931), p. 235.

111.   Hilgers, *The Catholic Encyclopedia*, "Sabbatine Privilege," vol. 13, p. 290.

112.   For an explanation of how the Roman Catholic Church fits the description of the woman in Revelation 17, see *A Woman Rides the Beast* by Dave Hunt (Eugene, OR: Harvest House Publishers, 1994).

113.   Quoted by Pope John Paul II, *Crossing the Threshold of Hope*, p. 146.

114.   Keith A. Fournier, *Evangelical Catholics* (Nashville, TN: Thomas Nelson Publishers, 1990), p. 65.

115.   Ibid., p. vi.

116.   Charles Colson, *The Body* (Dallas: Word Publishing, 1992), p. 265.

117.   Charles Colson and Richard John Neuhaus, *Evangelicals and Catholics Together: Toward a Common Mission* (Dallas: Word Publishing, 1995), p. xi.

118.   J. I. Packer, "Why I Signed It," *Christianity Today,* December 12, 1994, p. 35.

119.   Colson and Neuhaus, *Evangelicals and Catholics Together,* p. ix.

120.   Ibid., p. xiii.

121.   J. I. Packer, "Why I Signed It," *Christianity Today,* December 12, 1994, p. 36.

122.   Ibid.

123.   Ibid.

124.   *Catechism of the Catholic Church,* no. 882.

125.   Second Vatican Council, "Decree on Ecumenism," no. 4.

Subject Cross-Reference

Topic	Catechism of the Catholic Church (paragraph numbers)	The Gospel According to Rome (page numbers)
Act of Contrition	1430-39, 1451-54, 1492	73, 77
Acts of penance	1434-39, 1450-60, 1494	78-79, 83
Actual grace	2000, 2024	38, 56-57
Adoration of the Eucharist	1178, 1183, 1378-81, 1418, 2691	131-32, 143-44
Assumption of Mary	966, 974	188, 197, 203, 224, 281-84, 293-300
Attendance at Mass obligatory	1389, 1417, 2042, 2181	131
Baptism	403, 977, 1212-84, 1992, 2020	21-34, 323-32
Bible study	85, 100-41, 2653	276-80, 285-86, 301-03,
Bishops	880-96	234-35, 248-52
Ecumenism	817-22, 855	319-20
Grace by performance of a rite	1127-29	32, 64, 157-58
Grace lost through mortal sin	1033, 1855, 1874	75-76
Hail Mary	435, 2676-78	79, 206, 215
Hierarchical monarchy	771, 779, 880-87	234-61
Immaculate Conception	411, 490-93, 508	186-87, 196-97
Indulgences	1471-79, 1498	94-95, 206
Infallibility	889-92, 2032-35, 2051	79, 206, 215
Initial sanctifying grace	1262-74	26-28, 45-46, 55, 60, 112
Last Rites	1499-1532	89-91, 335
Liturgy and rites	1066-75, 1124-25	17-18, 236
Magisterium	77, 85-88, 100, 113, 861-62, 888-92, 2032-40, 2049-51	263-80
Mary	273, 411, 484-511, 618, 721-26, 773, 829, 963-75, 2030, 2617-19, 2622, 2673-82	95, 181-230, 293-300
Mass	1322-1419	125-77, 333
Merit	1021-22, 1036, 1038-41, 1051, 1053, 1821, 2010-11, 2016, 2027	95-103
Mortal and venial sin	1033, 1849-76	74-76, 84-86
Obligatory attendance at Mass	1389, 1412, 2042, 2181, 2192	130-31

Topic	Catechism of the Catholic Church (paragraph numbers)	The Gospel According to Rome (page numbers)
Original sin	388-89, 396-409, 415-19, 978, 1250, 1263, 1279	24-28
Peter	440-43, 552-56, 640-42, 765, 816, 862, 880-82, 1444	235-48, 252-61
Pope	552-53, 857-96, 1555-56	234-61
Real presence	1353, 1373-81	127-44, 151
Redemptive sufferings of mankind	618, 964, 1505, 1521, 1532	210-11, note 326
Religious titles		248-49
Roman Catholic Church as necessary for salvation	168-69, 824, 845-46, 1129	57, 64-65
Roman Catholic Church as the true church	811-70	12-13, 232-61
Rosary	971, 1674, 2678, 2708	58-59, 95, 205-06
Rule of Faith	80-85, 96-100, 182	286-87
Sacrament of confession	976-87, 1422-98	76-82, 334-35
Sacrament of the Eucharist	1322-1419	56-58, 62-68, 130
Sacramentals such as relics, the miraculous medal, and the scapular	1667-79	58-59
Sacraments	1113-34	56-69, 333-35
Sacred deposit of faith	84, 86, 97	285-86, 293-94
Sacrifice of the Mass	1085, 1323, 1330, 1353-54, 1362-72, 1382-83, 1409	148-74
Saints	828, 946-62, 2683-84	95, 194-95
Salvation by faith plus works	183, 1129, 1212, 1392, 1815-16, 1821, 2001-02, 2010	39-50, 69, 98, 100-03
Sanctifying grace	374-84, 1265-66, 1279, 1996-2000, 2023-24	26-28, 55-57, 62-65
Scripture and Tradition as the rule of faith	80-85, 96-100, 182	286-87
Separated brethren	818, 855, 1271	319
Sola Scriptura	82	287-307, 345-54
Statues and the second commandment	2129-32, 2141	278-80, endnote 465
Temporal punishment	1471-73, 1863	83-84, 92, 95
Threefold power of bishops	888-96	234-35, 248-52
Tradition	74-84, 96-98	284-309, 341-44
Uncertainty of salvation	1036, 1861, 2005	91-92, 104-07

Scripture Index

Subject Index

Altar cavity 154
Ankerberg, John 176
Authority (biblical)
    Holy Spirit as teacher 126
    Jesus is the Rock 121,122,123
    Sola Scriptura 125,126
Authority (Catholic) 116 (see also
    Bishops, Deposit of faith, Magisterium,
        Pope)
    apostolic succession 124,132
    bishops successors of apostles
        59,116,117
    growing challenges 118,119
    Magisterium 116,117,118,132
    Pope successor of Peter
        44,59,117,121,122,123,124,140
    Scripture and Tradition
        79,92,112,116,117,121,125,132,
        133,135
    submission to Rome 118,124

Baptism (biblical) 14
Baptism (Catholic) (see also *Sacraments)*
    cause of spiritual rebirth 14
    grace of justification 47
    infant 14,15,176
    two effects 14
Bernardin, Cardinal Joseph 120
Bible study (Catholic)
    136,137,138,157,163,164
Birth control 112,119,139
Bishops 78
    infallible 118,135
    relationship to pope 117
    three powers 116
    U.S. bishops divided 119
Brethren, separated 59,170
Bright, Bill 176
Bush, Bob 77,147,160

Cardinals 78
Catechism of the Catholic Church
    8,9,76,134,135,172,175,176,177,185,186
Catholicism: Crisis of Faith 40,47,48
Colson,Charles 174,175,176,177
Confession (see also *Sacraments)*
    absolution 18
    forgiveness of mortal sins 15
    and Last Rites 16
    penance assigned 18
Contrition, Act of 18,19,20,21
Council of Trent 75,76,172
Council, Second Vatican
    59,63,76,93,117,134,135,136,144,177,178
Crossing the Threshold of Hope 106,130
Curia, Roman 78

Deposit of faith 132,133,136,139

Ecumenism
    169,170,171,175,176,177,178,179
Eucharist (see also *Mass)*
    Blessed Sacrament 94
    body and blood of Christ 94,96,97
    communion 26,29,30,102
    Exposition of the Blessed Sacrament
        102,103
    host 91,103,104,110,155,163
    and Last Rites 26
    mystical reality 95
    necessary for salvation 95,97
    real presence 102
    sacrificial nature 95
    source of grace 94
    spiritual food 94
    thanksgiving 94
    transubstantiation 99,102
    worship of 94,103,136
Evangelicals and Catholics Together
    175,176,177
Excommunication 84,85
Exposition of the Blessed Sacrament
    102,103

Fiedler, Sister Maureen 119
Fournier, Keith 174

Gospel According to Rome
    8,9,82,106,185,186
Grace (biblical) 47
Grace, actual (Catholic)
    defined 26
    received through Eucharist 94
Grace, sanctifying (Catholic)
    brings into state of grace 14
    defined 26
    described 47
    earned 47
    effects upon soul 14
    initial grace is free 47
    initially received through baptism 14
    lost through mortal sin 26
    necessary for salvation 26
    received through Eucharist 94
    requirements to obtain and
        preserve 50

193

Printed in the United Kingdom
by Lightning Source UK Ltd.
127575UK00001B/80/A